"The Story Equation is pure genius." Randy Ingermanson, author of *Writing Fiction for Dummies*

"In simple yet powerful terms, Susan May Warren lays down the **essential crafting elements that make for a gripping tale.** This is the stuff we all need to first learn and then constantly keep in mind as we dive into the process of laying the story we see in our minds down on the page. A great benefit to all writers of fiction." Ted Dekker, *New York Times* best-selling author.

"There have been only two must-have craft books on my shelf for years. Now there is a third. **If you write fiction, Susan May Warren's** *The Story Equation* is a book you need to buy. And devour. I could talk in detail about the book's insight, its power to transform your writing, its brilliance, but suffice it to say I predict this will become a classic in the library of how to write bestselling stories." James L. Rubart, bestselling-author of *The Long Journey to Jake Palmer.*

"Susan May Warren loves to help novelists outrageously succeed. She does this in a practical way through her insightful book, *The Story Equation.* I felt like I'd been taken by the hand and mentored by a masterful storyteller!" Mary DeMuth, author of six novels including, *The Muir House.*

"Susan May Warren is a terrific teacher and enabler of fiction writers. I wholeheartedly agree with the approach of starting from the character journey and wrapping the plot around it. I think the SEQ can really help lots of authors." Jeff Gerke, national writing instructor and *Writer's Digest* author of *The Irresistible Novel.*

The Story Equation

Susan May Warren

MYBOOK🔥THERAPY

Minneapolis, Minnesota

learnhowtowriteanovel.com

The Story Equation: How to Plot and Write a Brilliant Story with One Powerful Question

Visit our Web site at www.learnhowtowriteanovel.com for information on more resources for writers.

To receive instruction on writing, or further help with writing projects via My Book Therapy's boutique fiction editing services, contact info@mybooktherapy.com.

It All Adds Up to a Powerful Story!

How can you take your writing to the next level? How do you add those rich layers and create constant tension that have your readers turning pages late at night and losing sleep? Whether you're published, seeking publication, or bravely navigating the new world of indie publishing, you need the Story Equation.

Ask yourself one powerful question and find the elements that add up to a compelling story. Fascinating characters, their internal and external journeys, story and scene tension, a riveting romance, and even the perfect ending are all connected components of best-sellers. The Story Equation is something every writer—novice or advanced, outliner or organic—can use.

Using this powerful technique that has helped me create nearly fifty books, many of which have landed on the best-seller list and won RITA, Carol, or Christy awards, I will ask the one question that leads to the Story Equation and then show you how to utilize it for the best story you've ever written.

You will discover:

•   The amazing trick to creating unforgettable, compelling characters that epic movies use

•   How to create riveting tension to keep the story driving from chapter to chapter

•   The easy solution to plotting the middle of your novel

•   The one element every story needs to keep a reader up all night

•   How to craft an ending that makes your reader say to their friends, "Oh, you have to read this book!"

Dedication:

For your Glory, Lord . . .

To everyone who ever attended one of my classes, encouraged me, and wanted more from their writing, this is for you.

Acknowledgements

To Rachel, my story therapist, my teaching partner and the person who said, "hey, what you teach sounds sort of like an equation."

You are brilliant.

To David, my amazing assistant for helping me sort out how to write this book, for his thoughtful questions and helping me each week teach these concepts to writers. I would be adrift without you.

To Beth Vogt, for your friendship and for applying your amazing editing skills to this book. I shudder to think what it would have looked like without you!

To the My Book Therapy Voices for their encouragement and questions that make me into a better writer and teacher.

Finally, to Andrew and my family.

Thank you for feeding me and keeping me sane. I love you guys.

Foreword

I've been writing partners with Susan May Warren, affectionately called Susie May, for more than a decade.

Her passion for writing and story is eclipsed only by her passion for teaching and mentoring.

In 2005, outside a Nashville coffee house, we brainstormed our current books. We found an instant connection and camaraderie. We laughed while challenging each other's story points and from that moment on, we grew in friendship and craft.

Over the years, Susie molded everything she learned into acronyms, how-to steps, and what to dos. I watched her heart to teach and mentor explode. Out of that came the multifaceted and brilliant My Book Therapy.

The book you hold in your hands, *The Story Equation*, is the result of ten plus years of writing, teaching, rewriting, and long phone conversations on how to tell a better story.

The methods and techniques you'll learn in the book are proven. Susie uses them. I use them. Award-winning authors trained through My Book Therapy use them.

Here's the thing, the SEQ is designed to work with your process. It's not a one, two, three step-by-step guide, but a tool box you can use to build your best possible story. The SEQ works for pantsers, plotters, and everyone in between.

Read this book over and over. Use it as a guide for each story you'll start. The techniques will become second nature to you. This will be one of the best writing books you've ever purchased.

Now, read. **Then go write something brilliant.**

Rachel Hauck, *New York Times*, *USA Today* and *Wall Street Journal* best-selling author

Introduction

The Job of the Author

It's all about story. No, wait. It's all about characters. Or what about the plot?

These comments are constantly batted around at writers conferences, in libraries, over mocha-lattes, and in book clubs. What makes a novel powerful, something you want to pass along?

All of the above. Because theme, plot, and characters all conspire to create the one thing a reader needs in order to enjoy—and pass along—a story.

The emotional connection.

Wouldn't it be nice if you could plot your entire story and create an emotional connection with your reader by asking one question?

You can. And that question is:

Who are you?

The answer to this question forms the core of the Story Equation, which is divided into two elements:

- Your character's Identity
- Your character's Dark Moment Story

From that Dark Moment Story (DMS) you're going to pull all your essential ingredients to create your compelling character and riveting plot:

- the character's Greatest Fear
- his Lie
- his Flaw
- his Competing Values
- his Want
- his Wound
- and the big Why that drives the entire story

Let me stop here and remind you what fundamental pieces a story needs. A sympathetic character who wants something for a good reason but has something to lose (a.k.a., the problem), who goes on a quest to attain that goal and solve that problem. He faces substantial internal and external obstacles and discovers he must change and grow to overcome them until he finds himself in a better place at the Happily Ever After ending.

How well your readers *connect with* and *care about* this character determines the success of a story. In other words, if they've emotionally gone on the journey with the character, suffered with and experienced the joys and triumphs of the character, as well as learned the lessons and truths, only then have you, the author, done your job.

In short, did you move your readers emotionally—make them laugh, cry, worry—so that they hated to put the book down?

Because if readers are emotionally invested in a story, they will be glued to the outcome, cheering for the characters, weeping with them when they fail, and ultimately learning the lessons the characters learned in the finale of the journey. And, in this way, your readers will be forever impacted by the story.

Drawing your reader into the story is accomplished by creating an emotional connection with the reader. If they *feel* and *live* the story, then they will like your story. Yes, it's important to write the words well because glaring grammar and punctuation errors, as well as poorly crafted sentences, pull readers out of a story and distance them. A smoothly written story and a well-crafted plot pull a reader in.

But ultimately, it's the universal emotional connection to the story that matters the most.

And it's this connection that causes stories to change lives forever—they are carried in the hearts of readers, passed from friend to friend, generation to generation, and ultimately make a mark on the world with the truths held inside.

Let's test this.

What stories have changed you? *To Kill a Mockingbird? A Christmas Carol? Little Women? The Adventures of Huckleberry Finn?* Think about the books you loved as a child. Did they empower you? Inspire you? Anger you? How did they shape your view of the world?

Did you read *The Shack?* Millions have read this book, and it touched people on a deep level, regardless of whether or not they agreed with the theology.

I was forever changed by Francine River's *Redeeming Love*, the rewritten biblical story of Hosea and Gomer. A romance, yes, and a fairly simple plot, but it was emotionally impacting to the point where it influenced my view not only of romance, but of God.

How about that for leaving a legacy?

And deep down, isn't this the desire of all authors? Sure, we want to make money, and we'd like our stories to be critically acclaimed, but at the end of the day, most authors would admit to wanting their books to be listed among those that matter most because they changed readers' lives.

The ones readers tally on their must-read lists.

So how do you create an authentic, powerful, emotional connection with a reader?

As an author, I'm always striving to improve my writing and to deepen that connection with my readers.

One might think that a great story has layers of characterization and devices hidden in the prose to tug at the readers' emotions. I've sat in classes and read books where the instructor suggests a 100-point checklist for building a character. My brain suddenly blows up, and I run in search of chocolate. Seriously? How do I even think of 100 things about a character?

And what does that have to do with the emotional connection and, more importantly, the Character Change Journey?

Thankfully, the answer to powerful storytelling is not found in making the stories and characters more complicated. Storycrafting and character building don't have to be mind-numbing and confusing.

In fact, they can be quite simple, and both start with one easy question.

This doesn't mean our stories or characters are simple, shallow, or mundane. Instead, getting at the heart of a character, crafting the plot around the character's journey, and helping the reader relate to the character are simplified.

As I developed my methods over the past decade of writing, I came upon a process that has helped me break down the storycrafting and characterization into one natural "equation".

In fact, you'll be shocked at how easy the process is. Simple. And it makes sense. Suddenly, storycrafting is unlocked.

You'll observe the Story Equation everywhere in books and movies (and probably drive your friends crazy as you analyze these stories).

In fact, I'd even call it *fun*.

I've named this method the Story Equation, but if math freaks you out like it does me, then delete the word Equation and think *diagram*. Or step-by-step ingredient list.

You can even call it the Story Donut if that helps. The key is, all the pieces start together. . .and add up to a fantastic story.

Let me show you how.

Section One
Making the Reader Care

The Four-Act Story

The key to building motivation, creating sympathy, and building the epic ending

As authors, if our job is to help a reader engage with the character, feel his journey, and triumph with him, how do we do this? It doesn't just happen—it takes a methodical, designed, step-by-step plan of action.

We can't just slap a character on the page, give him a few lines of expository backstory to explain the why, add stakes, and expect a reader to instantly care about him. Yes, those are the ingredients, but there is a process to falling in love with a character.

I'm going to teach you this *process*, the secret tricks to making your reader care . . . and it's all played out in what I call the **Four-Act Story**.

Popular writing teachers will say that a great book has three main acts:

- **Act 1**, or the setup of the story that contains the Inciting Incident.

- **Act 2**, where all the fun and games happen and the biggest character growth occur, driven by the challenges of the story. Act 2 cumulates in the Black Moment Event, or the advent of the *climax* of the story.

- **Act 3** is the grand finale. In Act 3, the hero overcomes his Greatest Fear, sees through the Lie he believes, embraces truth, and becomes a new man. It culminates with some grand gesture or sacrifice at the end that proves he's changed.

This is a fantastic and proven structure that authors use universally. In it, Act 1 and Act 3 can be fairly easy to plot. However, the problem arises in Act 2, or the "muddling middle."

The middle is the hardest portion of the story to write, mostly because it must contain, in a reasonable rhythm, everything needed to set up the character change of Act 3 as well as any romantic threads. Act 2 must build the suspense and create the theme of the story. And it must heighten the tension, raise the stakes, and set the character up for his Black Moment fall. Admittedly, so much occurs in Act 2 that an author can get tangled up in the details. Worse, an author might start writing in circles, rehashing old plot devices, never moving forward.

A Four-Act plot solves this problem by dividing Act 2 into two sections—Act 2A and Act 2B—with each section having its own purpose. To make it even easier, each of the Four-Act sections will have an emotional purpose—meaning the point of the four acts is to bring the character through his Character Change Journey step-by-step, with the right motivation for each choice. This ensures that the reader engages with each step, continuing the journey with the character through all the obstacles and challenges.

Remember, the goal of every story is to make the reader care about the character.

Before we dive into the structure of the Four-Act plot, however, let's look at the substance of each section, or the flow of character change and emotional connection with the reader.

By the way, we will talk about overall story structure. Let's talk about character change first, and then I'll show you how it fits into an external plot.

Act 1: Bio

The Character Change Journey

As an author, since your key job is to help readers identify with the character, feel his journey, and triumph with him, how do you do this?

In other words, how do you make a reader care about a character?

I hope you've seen the movie *Braveheart*, because I'll use it a bit to explain reader engagement. It's a movie constructed to resonate with both women and men, and it does a fantastic job of creating emotions despite the brutality of war on the screen.

William Wallace's character is a brutal, rough-edged warrior, and yet by the end, most women in the audience are weeping over him. Why?

It's because his journey is so heart-wrenching and poignant. The viewer knows where Wallace came from and what he's gone through, thus his ending is tragic. It is exactly right for his character because it accomplishes his Secret Desire and Goal.

But we need to back up and start with the *Why*.

The Bio Story

good point {

I am hesitant to use the term "backstory" because it is misused in books. Authors often employ a "backstory dump" as a narrative tool to tell the reader about the character instead of allowing the character to reveal himself on the page. This misses the purpose of backstory, and can turn your readers off of the story when they've hardly begun.

So we'll call it the Bio story instead, or the character biography, something we, the authors, will gather before we begin as a way to build our heroes.

Like much of the SEQ, Point of View (POV) characters each need their own bio. We're just talking about the protagonist's bio right now, but you should develop one for each POV character.

William's Bio story begins in the prologue, or opening scene, of *Braveheart* when his entire clan—his father, brothers, and cousins—are murdered by the English. At the funeral of his family, right before his uncle takes him away to be raised in a different village, a local girl takes pity on him and gives him a clover.

It's a kind act that William carries with him to adulthood. We discover later that he has kept the clover and pressed it in a handkerchief.

The current story begins with William returning to his father's village with the hope of rebuilding his family farm. He also meets the girl, now a grown woman, who had gifted him with the flower, and he falls in love with her.

They marry in secret, and everything seems to be heading toward a happy ending (and a swift ending to the movie), when the English harass his wife and end up killing her. *Aha!* This is the Inciting Incident for William's journey toward freeing his people from English rule.

And, of course, we instantly feel sorry for him again. Not only that, but we're furious about this tragedy, and have no qualms about joining with William on his quest for freedom. The Bio story has hooked us enough to entice us on the journey.

The power of the Bio story is to compel the reader or movie viewer to be sympathetic toward the POV character just enough to agree with the journey he must take.

In short, we care about him and are hooked to journey with him at least into Act 2.

A Bio story can be delivered in many ways. Occasionally it is revealed in a prologue. I don't recommend this, as it is the least effective use of the Bio story. Another method is to have it shown in action and explained as an aside to the character's behavior. Again, this is not the strongest way to deliver the Bio story.

The best way to reveal a Bio story is to drop breadcrumbs of information in the beginning chapters, or scenes, to stir the hunger of the reader. Your goal as the author is to raise intrigue about the character. You do this by scattering nibbles of dialogue or action that hint at a greater story, perhaps a conversation or a situation that suggests more.

But don't stop the story to give us backstory! That's going backward to tell us a story. Backstory stops the forward movement in a story and stalls the momentum in your book. If you tell the entire Bio story at the beginning, you've thrown away one of your most powerful tools for pulling the reader into the story.

Think about that delicious moment, usually early in Act 2, where the hero tells his story to someone else. It's that moment when the story stakes begin to feel real to the reader. (We'll talk about that more when we dive into the Dark Moment Story.) If you tell the story too early, you've wasted that momentum and have less to talk about in Act 2. You need all the power you can in Act 2 to keep things going.

The Bio story functions as the *Why* behind your character's actions, values, decisions, and dialogue—and discovering that *Why* is part of the fun for the reader. Think of it this way: in Act 1, you'll be *showing* the readers all the flaws, fears, lies, and desires of the character, whetting your readers' appetite to understand Why. In Act 2, you'll reward them for hanging in there by telling them the story behind the actions.

But you need to build the Bio story to know what actions and dialogue to give your character that reveal his fears, lies, flaws, and desires, right?

Act 1 and the hints of the Bio story only give your readers enough thrust to get them past the Inciting Incident and onto the journey. Once there, readers must decide if they are ready to face the challenges of Act 2. This problem is solved by Act 2A, the Cause.

Act 2A: The Cause

Why is your hero on this journey?

As your character moves into Act 2, he will face immediate obstacles to his goal. If accomplishing his goal were easy, then it wouldn't be a journey, right? These obstacles might be so big the poor guy just wants to turn around and go home. Don't let him!

Give your character a good reason to keep going.

Your character's motivation is his Noble Quest, his goal, his purpose for the journey. Remember, the entire point of your character's journey is to change and grow. The external plot exists to push him forward into that inner growth.

This is not unlike our own lives. Don't our external circumstances cause us to change who we are on the inside? And that change is often reflected in external ways, just like it will be for your character.

William Wallace's Noble Quest is to free Scotland from England's control. And because of William's Bio story, as well as the Inciting Incident—his wife's murder—we empathize with this quest.

The key to building a powerful Noble Quest is to convince the reader that it is a *worthy cause through the eyes of the POV character.* Even if readers aren't particularly inspired by the quest, if they can sympathize with the POV character and agree that he has a reason to pursue it, they will stay with the story.

We develop and strengthen the Noble Quest by building the *Cause* behind it. And we'll be diabolical and use specific tools designed to nudge your character—and reader—forward in the story. We'll dive deeper into these tools when we dissect the Four-Act Plot. Tools like giving your character a taste of victory—and defeat. We'll give your character a glimpse of his reward and a solid reality check by showing him the stakes. Finally, we'll unearth his greatest hidden desire.

The point of building the Cause is to arm the character—and reader—with enough motivation to face the next step in the journey: the Fight. The Cause reminds us of the stakes, helps the character see the value of his Noble Quest, and uses the Bio story as the grand motivator. Finally, it sets up the character for the most important moment in the story: the extra push into the fray of the Character Change Battle, or the Fight.

The Fight

There's no triumph without a fight!

Are you a sports fan? I'm a die-hard football fan. Can we agree that the best sporting events are those in which the team has to fight for the win? When the game is close and the fans are on their feet fearing a loss or cheering the underdogs to victory, we are engaged, right? A great fight causes players and fans to dig deep to discover what they really want and brings out the depths of passion and emotion to win the battle.

This is the makeup of the next step in the emotional journey for your character. During the Fight stage, your character confronts external obstacles that cause him to dig deep and take a look at himself. He'll have to examine his values, come to terms with his secret desires, and realize what he must sacrifice in order to achieve his goal.

The Fight section causes your character to change course, take risks, embrace new truths, and try new ideas in order to become the person he must be to accomplish his goals. This is where he begins to change.

And it is in this stage where readers are unequivocally, emotionally connected. The harder the fight is and the more the hero has to sacrifice for it, the more the reader will be on board, rooting for your character. We rally to the underdogs, and a great hero is always the underdog by the second half of Act 2. He has to fight his way to the castle, fight to rescue the girl, fight to save the town, and even wrestle with his own demons if he wants to save the earth from doom. Moreover, the fight must be big and overwhelming and must cost the character something.

During the Fight stage in *Braveheart*, William Wallace rallies all the Scottish lairds and goes to battle. Some of the battles he wins, but there are costs. He must change tactics, start to trust people. In each battle, he learns something along the way and makes new decisions, and the stakes are raised until he reaches that pinnacle moment where, just when he thinks he will triumph, his greatest fears come true.

This is called the Black Moment Event and happens at the end of Act 2B. It's a death of his hopes, dreams, and ultimately, the man he was. Without a Black Moment Event, you can't finish your Character Change Journey and thus, your story won't have a satisfying ending.

Why? When our worst fears come true, we look back and ask, *Why did this happen?* And at that moment we are forced to confront the lies we believe, our broken behaviors (flaws), and our fears. This is called the Black Moment Effect, which we'll talk more about next. Hopefully in that moment, we see the Truth. And so does your character.

The Truth causes the Epiphany, which occurs in the Resurrection stage of the journey.

As you're constructing your story, every decision your character makes will draw him closer to the Black Moment Event and thus to the low point in his journey, we call the Black Moment Effect. The old version of him will die . . . and be resurrected into the new to finish his story.

Act 3: Resurrection and Triumph

It's all about how we finish.

We cheer and feel good about movies where the hero triumphs.

But triumphing isn't that easy. A hero can't triumph as the person they were before. The very point of the journey is to become someone new, learn new lessons, gain new skills, and leave the story better than he began it.

However, before your character can triumph, he must be brought to his knees in defeat during the Black Moment Event when his Greatest Fear comes true. In that moment, he believes a Lie and feels like a failure. We'll talk about this more when we discuss the Lie Journey.

Believing the Lie is called the Black Moment Effect. It is strong enough to crush the hero, make him want to run for home, believe he is defeated.

It is at this moment that your character, as we know him, dies. Only by bringing your character to his knees will a change occur. It is here, at his weakest moment, that your hero looks back along the journey and discovers the truthlets that have been dropped along the road, and suddenly, the character realizes: *This is the purpose of my story.* The external events have conspired to push him forward, make him change, see truth, and help him realize that if he wants to triumph, he'll have to break free of his Lie, hold onto the Truth, and become a New Man.

It's this new man who rises from the Black Moment as a result of his Epiphany and goes forward to accomplish his final goal.

To prove that your character has changed, he will do something at the end of the story that he couldn't do at the beginning. He'll make a Grand Gesture, sacrifice something, engage in a Final Battle. In the end, the reader will experience the grand finale and triumphant ending that leaves them with a feeling of victory.

It is this feeling that will make an impact and linger, inspiring your reader to pass along your book to others.

Hopefully, your character's lessons will also be taken to heart by the reader. That's how you nudge the world with your words!

William Wallace's Black Moment is when he is betrayed by one of his kinsman. It's a devastating blow—his own man turned against him, and he is captured by English forces. In that moment, he fears that he has done *nothing*, that all his fighting is for naught, that Scotland will never be free, especially if her own people don't fight for her. However, his Epiphany is his realization that he can still inspire, can still rally his fellow Scots to freedom by his noble, brave death.

Remember when we talked about William's secret desire? His Bio story? His Why? William Wallace returned home to build a life and legacy. And although his wife died, he inspired Scotland with his bravery and ultimately led the charge to freedom. In this way, he also honored the memory of his murdered family and wife.

This is how readers fall in love with a character. They understand who he is and, as the story progresses, they get on board with his cause, they cheer for him through the fight, feel his defeat at the Black Moment, and then triumph with him in the end.

When your readers close the book, that triumphant feeling causes them to want to tell someone—and pass the book along. They are so emotionally connected they want others to feel the same triumph.

And you, the author, stand on the sidelines, cheering!

A Storycrafter Challenge

It's your turn. Now that you've seen the breakdown of the Four-Act plot, it's time to test it. Take out a few of your favorite movies and divide them into Four Acts. Remember, Act 2A begins with the character's launch into the Noble Quest. Act 2B starts midway through the movie when the character decides to fight for what he wants. The Black Moment Event occurs at the end of Act 2B, and bridges into Act 3 with the Black Moment Effect.

Act 3 is all about the Epiphany, New Man, and Final Battle (or climax of the story).

We'll talk about external story structure and all the components of the internal story structure (Lie and Character Change Journey) in Section 3, but for now, let's move onto the Story Equation and learn how to create a character from the inside out, pulling out all those pieces we'll need to build the Four Acts and the Character Change Journey.

Would you like a free infographic and 1-hour lesson on how to build a powerful character?

Check out our Story Equation Mini-Course!
(http://novel.academy/courses/TheSEQ/)

The SEQ Diagram

Section Two
Building the SEQ

Why an Equation?

"Oh no, an **equation**! Why do I have to do math to tell a story?"

You don't. Instead, I want you to think of ingredients.

The Story Equation (SEQ) is a recipe. Consider a chocolate chip cookie recipe. You need flour, eggs, sugar, brown sugar, baking soda, salt, and chocolate chips. Without any of these ingredients, you have a cookie-like substance, but it wouldn't be a real cookie.

You could say that all these ingredients add up to a great cookie. A cookie equation, if you will.

We're going to create an equation of ingredients that add up to a great story.

But why use such a regimented equation or list? Some would say that you should simply be able to "feel" your way into a great story.

Sometimes simply opening your cupboard and throwing ingredients together can have a great outcome, but getting it right every time requires a very special person with the experience to "feel" their way through. But long before any great chefs were cooking masterpieces with their intuition, they began simply. They followed recipes, experimented, and learned how everything works. Even if you prefer not to plan ahead, this SEQ can help you.

Whether or not you enjoy having an ingredient list, the SEQ gathers up all the ingredients of a cohesive story. It lets you plan ahead, so that you don't have to struggle to develop your story. At first glance it might feel overwhelming, but once you understand all the elements, the storycrafting process with the SEQ becomes not only simplified, but organic, all the way through to the satisfying happy ending.

The SEQ Is Simple

The reality is that a great story has many layers. An author steps into the story thinking: "I'll simply start with goals, motivation, and conflict. That's easy . . . Oh, but wait. Now I have to have a Black Moment, and what is this about a Dark Moment Story? I have to have a Lie? What do you mean my character needs a Flaw? He has to have a Noble Quest and an Inner Journey? I can't do an Epiphany *and* a Grand Gesture. Come on. How much do you want from me?"

All of it. We want all of it. But yes, it can be overwhelming to think about all these things. You can get buried in those layers, trying to conjure up another element in the great storycrafting list.

The SEQ eliminates this by helping you build each layer, step-by-step, in a logical, organic, character-driven way.

But the SEQ goes beyond this to help you build the three essential journeys: The External (Plot) journey, the Internal (Spiritual) journey, and the Character Change Journey (the glue that connects the External journey to the Internal journey).

The SEQ Is Organic

How many of you have ever downloaded a list of 100 things you need to create for your character? You can be honest, I won't judge you. I have.

You can now delete it from your computer! [Applause!] You don't need the list anymore because you're going to learn to create a character from the inside out.

The SEQ is organic. It's something that feels logical, natural. With the SEQ, you're suddenly creating a character without a list of crazy, this-has-nothing-to-do-with-the-story questions like:

- What kind of car does he drive?

- What is your character's favorite food?

- What music does he listen to?

- Does he have a pet?

The SEQ doesn't ask these questions because *they don't matter to the core of a story.* Instead, the SEQ asks:

- What does your character want and why?

- What is his compelling dilemma?

- What is his Noble Quest and what stands in his way?

More, it dives deep into character change, Epiphany, and finally, that grand thing your character does at the end that he can't do at the beginning.

Logical, yet powerful questions.

The SEQ is Powerful

A character who isn't properly motivated is a character who loses power in the middle of the story. More, a character who doesn't have the right motivation is a weak, namby-pamby character we can't love. When authors see this at the midpoint of their novel, they start to panic, and then "plotter's brain" takes over, convincing authors that they have to make their characters behave *because that's what the plot requires.* This is why we see characters suddenly doing things "out of character" or making lousy, plot-driven decisions, as opposed to logical, character-driven decisions.

The SEQ aligns your character's actions with his motivation. This is essential because readers must understand and believe in a character's motivation if they want to agree with their actions. Even if they don't agree, they understand and empathize with his actions. In other words, if readers understand why the characters are doing what they're doing and they know those characters have a good reason for it, it doesn't matter what they do, they're going to say, "Yes, this is a good idea."

The SEQ starts from the middle, or the core, of the character and builds out, thus establishing the correct—and most powerful—motivation from the start. In this way, every decision is created with the correct motivation behind it, making that decision logical and organic.

The point of the SEQ is to produce authentic, developed, and layered characters who are properly and powerfully motivated without using a list.

The SEQ Is Satisfying

When we know what our character wants and why, what drives him, and what he deeply desires, we, as authors, can build a satisfying Happily Ever After (HEA) ending.

The SEQ helps you create the perfect HEA ending. It's not enough to let your character catch the villain, get married, and ride off into the sunset. The perfect HEA ending involves *healing deep emotional wounds* and *realizing greatest dreams and desires*. The SEQ probes into your character's past to help discover these elements, giving you a target to aim at while building the story.

Even if you are not a plotter or a planner, if you like pulling out whatever ingredients you have and throwing together the cookie that tempts you, the SEQ can build a framework to give you direction as you launch out onto your journey.

The Sympathetic Character

The Key to a Brilliant Novel

Before we start into the SEQ and why it's key to begin with character, let's talk about the debate between character-driven and plot-driven novels.

Character-Driven Versus Plot-Driven Novels

Think of the last book you read, the last movie you watched. Even your favorite television series.

Were you more interested in the plot or the people? I would bet that the element that drew you into the story was the characters.

Let's think about this. Plot is interesting, but if we don't care about the characters, the story will lose us quickly. A fantastic example is *The Hunger Games.* The plot construction and premise are fantastic: a dystopian world where one district makes the other districts pay for their rebellion and earn their food allotment by making two champions from each district fight for their survival. Interesting and tragic, but not compelling . . . until a champion rises. And not just one champion, but two: one who loves the other and both who choose to defy the system—and they inadvertently start a revolution toward freedom.

The Hunger Games is interesting, but it's the compelling fight for survival of the champions that makes both the book and the series riveting.

Another great example is the *Firefly* series, a sci-fi about Mal, a captain renegade smuggler, who is trying to survive in an unforgiving universe. As the TV show progresses, we care about Mal and his crew as they struggle to stay alive and save the life of a girl who is on the run. When they encounter peril, we care because we want Mal and his crew to survive.

The key to this series, however, is that we understand Mal's past, what drives him, the wounds he carries, his greatest fears, and his great loyalty to his crew. We also know that this group of people has survived a war together. Without this insight, we'd simply think: *It's just another space adventure.* This is the point of a great television series—the people we care about.

There is really no such thing as a book driven exclusively by plot. It would read like a history textbook. All books are about *characters*. Your plot just serves to push your character forward. You can have some powerful, interesting external stakes, but we don't care about them unless it gets personal.

The movie *Independence Day* isn't only about saving the world. It's also about bringing home pilots Steven Hiller and David Levinson, the computer geek, to their loved ones, as well as redeeming Russell Casse and finding justice for President Whitmore.

Even in a nuclear war plot, the reader will be asking: *What is the character doing?* He's trying to save a village. He's trying to save the government. You, the author, want him to succeed because you want life to go on. So at its core, despite the external stakes, your story is really about Joe, who is going to save the world from nuclear holocaust. And you'll need to develop Joe so your reader will care.

Let's quickly recap what we learned in Section One: Making the Reader Care. Remember that you should be using this process for both your hero and heroine, as well as any additional POV characters. In my examples, I'll be using the hero as an example, but these story principles are equally valid with a heroine as well.

Overview of Story

A great story is about a character who we care about who wants something for good reason. This hero is driven by some sort of Dark Moment Story in his past that has propelled him forward into the person he is as he walks onto the page.

The hero also has a Fear about something that he's trying to avoid while he's going about his normal life.

Then something happens. This something, called the Trigger or the Inciting Incident, creates a compelling Dilemma that he must solve. Either to put right what went wrong or to pursue something positive that is now necessary. This is called the Noble Quest—a worthy, justifiable goal. Restated, he either has something negative that happens and he needs to pursue a positive outcome or he has something positive that happens and he wants to keep that positive outcome and not lose it again.

This is also where the Secret Desire starts tapping on his heart. It's that deep want, sparked by his Dark Moment Story that starts to fuel the Noble Quest. The Noble Quest is always articulated through an external goal. However, it's driven by that internal Desire, the *Why*. The most powerful motivation for the Noble Quest is a combination of something that the hero wants based on his Secret Desire and something negative that happened in the past that he doesn't want to repeat.

Thus motivated, he launches on his journey, whether it be physical or metaphorical. While the character has an external, physical goal, the journey itself—the entire story, really—is about character growth. The point of the story, or Noble Quest, is for the hero to overcome his flaws, be set free of his fears, heal his wounds, and become a new person at the end.

The character journey culminates in the Black Moment Event—or the realization of his Greatest Fear. As a result of this event, he experiences a Black Moment Effect when the Lie that has been chasing him the entire book suddenly feels real. This Black Moment Effect drives him to his metaphorical knees where he experiences an Epiphany.

This Epiphany, or realization of the point of his journey, contains some universal truth that sets him free, transforms him, and gives him the tools to do something at the end that he couldn't do at the beginning, such as fighting the Final Battle.

He is also able to overcome his Flaw in a moment of Grand Gesture or Sacrifice.

If your character hasn't had a Black Moment, an Epiphany, and a Character Change, then he hasn't completed his journey.

Figuring out how to construct this internal Character Change against the backdrop of external goals can admittedly be overwhelming.

So we don't start with turning on the mixer and randomly tossing things in... First we assemble our SEQ ingredients.

Who = Dark Moment Story

Start with Who and Why to Build the Powerful Dark Moment Story

At the beginning of this book, I asked you the question you're going to use to plot your whole story. That question was: *Who are you?*

We've talked about the Four-Act Plot, which is like the box you sell your cookies inside. It's absolutely vital, but it isn't why anyone buys your story. Now let's get to the good stuff!

Who are you?

The SEQ starts by asking the character, *"Who are you?"* Often we bring to the novel what we call the story seed. This is the original idea that sparked a big question, a situation, a historical figure or event, even a great what-if—it's probably from something we've heard or read.

For our storycrafting purposes, let's start with the idea, or seed, of writing a story about a female billionaire. Let's say she's made her fortune online—perhaps a dating website she created with her friends. The twist is that although she can find love for thousands or even millions, she and her three friends can't find it for themselves.

That's all we have. Once we have that story seed, we set it aside and let it grow on its own as we develop our character. Before we develop the plot, however, we have to ask: *Who is in this story?*

Let's start with our main character. Remember: You'll need to do the SEQ on every POV character and every other character who has a significant Character Change Journey.

The first question to ask your characters is: *Who are you right now?* Or you, as the author, can step back and ask: *As I see my characters, who are they right now?*

The key to this process is to keep it simple and find a powerful, interesting adjective, and a distinct noun. Noun + Adjective = Title The adjective reveals his emotional state. The noun gives us a physical place to build traits, skills, and competency. You'll build your character by digging down into this adjective and noun.

So, our POV character is a . . . broken billionaire.

We're going to drill down in a moment, but let's try this on a few of our favorite movies.

Who is William Wallace from *Braveheart?* A wounded warrior.

How about Forest Gump? A simple-minded hero.

How about Rose from *Titanic?* She's an imprisoned heiress.

Once you have decided on your adjective and noun, we need to drill down both descriptors by asking *Why.*

Why is our POV a broken billionaire? She's a billionaire, so she's not broken financially. She's got all this money, so she can do everything she wants to help her family or pursue her dreams, but there's something broken on the inside. Perhaps it's something she doesn't believe about the very business that she has built.

Let's keep asking *Why.* She has a dating business, but she doesn't believe it will work for her. Why does she believe that? Maybe she's never experienced love, she's never seen love. Or no matter what she tries, she can't find the satisfaction that she once had, perhaps back in the past. Maybe she had love, but she gave it up for her business, and she's never been able to find it again.

Let's keep asking *Why*.

What if she has been too afraid to try her own methods because she fears she can't find a match? Maybe the love of her life told her that dating isn't an equation but a twist of fate, and she doesn't believe in fate. Or faith. Or even, really, the one, true soul mate.

Why?

Perhaps she had a true love, but he cheated on her, and since then she's been jaded. She believes that it is better to depend on a formula than to trust her heart.

Oh, interesting . . . so now we have to ask her: *Tell me a time when you got hurt trusting your heart.*

Suddenly, you have the makings for a powerful Dark Moment Story (DMS) that will fuel your entire Character-Change Journey.

Let me show you how this works from one of my own books.

Owen Christiansen: Troublemaker

One of my favorite characters to develop was the final character in my Christiansen family series, Owen's book: *You're the One That I Want*. I'd already explored all his siblings, but I had no idea who Owen, the family troublemaker, was until I got to his story.

I needed an SEQ.

My conversation with Owen went something like this:

Who are you?

"I'm a prodigal fisherman."

Why are you a prodigal fisherman?

"I'm a fisherman because this is the job that I could get. I'm working on a crabbing boat. It's a short-term job, temporary. I don't have to commit to it. I can just work hard for a season, get money, and go on, because I'm a vagabond. I'm on the run from my past . . . hence, why I'm called a prodigal."

Is that the only reason you're a prodigal?

"Well no. I also made a terrible mistake and can't go home again."

Why can't you go home?

"I sort of made a mess of things at my sister's wedding when I was visiting."

Really, what happened?

"My brother Casper freaked out on me and attacked me in the middle of the wedding, and we got in a huge fistfight. I don't know what his problem was. Or . . . actually, I do. Apparently he fell in love with this girl that, okay, yes, I had a one-night stand with. I realized it was probably a bad thing, but I did it anyway. He fell in love with her, and when he found out we'd slept together, he took it personally and got angry. I probably didn't handle it well."

Why did you handle it badly? And, Owen, why did you sleep with this girl?

"I've had a rough go of it because I—you might not know this about me but—I used to be a professional hockey player. I was on top of my game, and then, well, my brother-in-law hit me with a hockey stick in my eye, and I lost vision in that eye. My whole career was destroyed. I had this life, and now I don't anymore. So thank you very much. This is my life now."

Perfect. Now, as an author, I have a little picture of Owen. I also have a hint of the DMS, which is the accident that caused him to lose his eye.

I can also build on that and easily ask: *What is his Greatest Dream and Secret Desire?* He wanted to play hockey. He wanted to be somebody.

Now that I've mined the adjective, I'll move over to the noun.

Fisherman. This gives me a hint of what Owen looks like on the outside. He's got an eye patch because he lost his sight in one eye. And he's working the high seas, so we can attach a pirate vibe to him. He's probably a hard worker because he needs to earn money. He might also be a bit unkempt, with a scruffy beard from being at sea for a month. He doesn't really care what he wears—old T-shirt, old sweatshirt, that sort of thing.

We can go even deeper and ask: *What's his attitude?* Who is this guy who's now working on a fishing boat? A person who's named himself a prodigal probably has a little bit of regret. When the story opens, Owen knows he's not doing the right thing, but he feels like there's no way back. He probably wears a small chip on his shoulder and most likely feels very alone. Perhaps he feels that he can't get close to people because he feels guilty about hurting his brother—which means he might even regret his womanizing ways. Perhaps he's even tried to amend his actions but still feels like he can't go home.

However, based on this analysis, his Secret Desire is definitely to go home. And we feel sorry for him.

Give Us a Dark Moment Story

The goal of this questioning is to get to the heart of your character by asking *Why* until you land on a definitive Dark Moment Story. We often refer to this as the DMS.

The DMS is the core of your SEQ; it's the secret sauce behind all the stuff that your character does. The DMS gives your character motivation, and it helps us determine his secret or Greatest Desire, which then helps us establish what he wants. This desire fuels his decision to embark on the Noble Quest. The DMS also establishes his Lie and helps develop your character's Flaw. In short, all the pieces of your SEQ come from this DMS.

We can find a DMS in almost every great movie.

As we discussed earlier, in *Braveheart*, William Wallace's DMS is played out in the first twenty minutes of the film. First, his family dies and then his wife, the woman he loves, dies.

In *While You Were Sleeping*, one of my favorite movies, the DMS is seen in the opening scenes as Lucy talks about her father, the stories he told her, and the dream he gave her to see the world. Later, Lucy tells pieces of this to Jack during their walk home through Chicago. She talks about how her father always wished to go somewhere but he got sick, and she had to take care of him.

The DMS can happen as far back as in childhood, more recently, or even as the first scene on the page. And the DMS is different and unique for every character.

If you are developing a continuing character through multiple books, your character will have a different DMS for each book, or some variation of the DMS that you can use to create a unique Black Moment for every book.

The creation of the DMS is exactly what you need to create the capstone of your novel: The Black Moment Event. This moment is not only the climax of the story but also is the point of change for your character and sets up the epic finale of your novel.

The Three Essential Elements to a Dark Moment Story

The secret power to the DMS is embodied in three things.

First, the DMS must be a specific event. Often, when authors develop a hero, they sum up his past with an overview: His parents got divorced or his mother died or his brother ran away or he was bullied in school . . . These are certainly traumatic, life-changing events, but none of them clues us in to how that event shaped your character. As an author, you have to create a specific event in which that seed of rejection, fear, unforgiveness, or bitterness was planted.

The DMS needs to be something that happened, something the character remembers, and something he can tell in detail. And often, the story isn't the main traumatic experience but an ancillary event that really matters.

It's not the moment when your character's mother died but six months later, when all the kids' mothers brought homemade Halloween cookies to school and he had store-bought Oreos. It's not all those days he got bullied but the one time when he fought back and ended up with a broken tooth and two weeks in detention for fighting.

Frequency, another of my favorite movies, is completely built off the power of a DMS. It's a time-travel movie about a man whose father died when he was a boy. Through the magic of a sun spot and an old ham radio, he is able to contact his father through time and warn him of his impending death.

The key element here is that his father's death has deeply affected the son and turned him into a cop instead of a firefighter, which was his father's profession, and made him unable to have long-lasting relationships (his Flaw). The hero's DMS is his memory of the funeral and hearing about his father's terrible death in a fire. He remembers the fire with such great detail that he is able to tell his father later—in the twist of time-travel fate—and help him craft a different ending. His father is able to avert disaster . . . and save lives.

The son is thrilled until, through a quirky turn of events, his mother suddenly dies in the past at the hands of a serial killer, and he wakes to an entirely different nightmare. Now he must reach back into time and help his father solve the murder of his mother before it happens.

In both cases, the DMS—first his father's death, then his new memory of his mother's funeral—is key to understanding and changing the future and ultimately healing him of his Flaw, helping him build relationships, and giving him his Greatest Dream: a family.

The Dark Moment Story Is Relatable

The second element of the DMS is that **it must be an event that readers can relate to**. You're looking for something poignant, something that will tug on the heartstrings of your audience. It doesn't have to be elaborate or even profoundly dramatic. It could merely be the day when no one showed up to your character's seventh birthday party. Or the day your character thought he was going fishing with his father and he got left at home. Sure, it might be powerful—the death of a family member, for example. But often we jump to the dramatic when, in fact, it's the small things that wound so deeply.

It might be an overheard conversation that changes the way a character looks at her life. Or perhaps a mistake that left an indelible mark on the hero, like the time when he accidentally set the garage on fire. Or even a failure in a sporting event. Anything that changes your character at his core, in his thinking, and behavior.

Be creative, and don't just jump at the first, logical event, but dig deeper and ask: *So when you caught the garage on fire, what lesson did you learn, and when did you really feel the impact of that lesson?*

Maybe it was when he realized he also burned the family car, and they had to walk eight miles to town for milk.

Whatever the case, it must be something readers can relate to. We might not understand the impact of a father giving the family riches to our hero's youngest brother, but we certainly understand what it feels like to be ignored and overlooked. That feeling of being unappreciated when the rascal younger brother returns home to fanfare and we're stuck in the hot fields, weeding the garden. Or in the kitchen, eating leftovers of the fatted calf.

Look for a story your readers will understand and relate to.

The Dark Moment Story Is Poignant

A powerful DMS is one that you, as the author, feel first. If in the telling of the story, your heart is moved for your character, then you're on the right track. Have your hero tell it to you in first person, and write it down in detail so you can hear and feel the inflection of his voice, his words, his emotion. (I do realize that sentence sounds a little schizophrenic, but you know what I mean.)

I want to emphasize how important it is to write the DMS down in detail. Even if I know the story in my head, I find that when I take the time and really interview the character and talk about that moment and dig in and get some responses from him, I get so much more nuance and material to work with. From experience,

I've discovered that if you don't write it down in detail, then you won't have enough ingredients or enough substance to understand every component.

Perhaps it goes without saying, but the DMS also needs to be a story. With a beginning, middle, and end.

Once the DMS is written down, you as the author, can take a look at it, and you can pull out the other ingredients that you're going to need for your SEQ. You'll be able to sense your hero's real, deep Fear. His Lie. The Wound (the emotional response to the story), and the Secret Desire that is birthed from it. Your DMS will be poignant, personal, and unique.

The magic of the DMS isn't just in developing your character; it's also a tool you'll use in the story to develop the bond between characters and between the hero and the reader.

Like Jack and Lucy in *Sleepless in Seattle* walking home together. Because when we tell each other our stories, even in written form on the page, we hear each other's hearts, and it is a bonding moment. We begin to care. And it's not just a device used in romances. Consider the bond between Roger Murtaugh and Martin Riggs in *Lethal Weapon*.

In most cases, you'll insert that story in dialogue in Act 2A to help solidify the Cause— motivation for the Noble Quest—as well as build the Character Change Journey. Yes, you might modify the story in the retelling on the page, but getting the foundation down now is the key.

Once you have your Identity and your DMS figured out, you have the tools to build the rest of the SEQ.

Now that you know who your character is and what motivates him, we can start to pull out a plot that will bring him to his knees.

The Power of the Greatest Fear

The Black Moment Event Hinges on Understanding Your Character's Greatest Fear.

Want to create powerful Character Change? Then you have to shake your character to the core of his being—essentially "kill" the old him and resurrect him as a New Man. And you do this by-the-hour causing his greatest fears to come true and making him believe his lies so he can reexamine them and realize life-giving truth.

This means that every character has to possess a deep and abiding Greatest Fear based on his DMS that has molded him as a person and helped establish motivation for all his decisions and choices. This Greatest Fear, as the novel opens, helps determine what your character wants (namely, not ever repeating this Greatest Fear) and guides his personality.

Let's build on Owen Christiansen. We already established that his DMS was when he lost his vision in one eye and his hockey career—essentially losing everything he had. So, based on that, what would his Greatest Fear be? Probably losing even more—truly losing everything. Thus, his greatest fears were realized when he got into the fight with his brother, caused a rift in his family, and realized how alone he truly was. He's gone beyond "I have alienated my fan base" to "I've lost my family." So knowing this, what would be a possible Black Moment for him? Perhaps never being able to reconcile with his family? Especially, perhaps, with his brother, with who he was once close?

The key to having a Greatest Fear is that you want to create something that could possibly happen again, maybe not with the same people or even the same event, but something that creates the same painful, emotional scenario. Maybe Owen again alienates someone he loves and there's no repair in sight. Or he destroys the one relationship he has left.

We might even take that deeper and have him fear that he a person who destroys relationships.

This is how every character turns out differently. You, as the author, get to build your own unique character, complete with his own wounds. Your character's reaction to that family fight might be different than another character's reaction to a family fight. The SEQ ensures that every character is uniquely different because his core makeup is unique.

No matter what DMS you create, it will produce an array of fears to choose from. Owen might fear getting hurt again. Or he might fear being betrayed by someone he loves, e.g., his family or a teammate. You can pick any fear you want out of that DMS. It all depends on what you want to do in your story and what story you want to tell.

The interesting part to storycrafting is that often we pick a fear we relate to, which means that we will have a truth in our past that we can then apply to the story. Now we're creating characters that we can tap into in an authentic way!

In *My Foolish Heart*, I created Izzy, a heroine who was agoraphobic. The story was based on a talk show host who's never been in love and was trapped in her home. The reason she was trapped in her home was because she had panic attacks as a result of having seen her parents die in a horrific car accident right outside their home.

I did not understand my character. I knew her DMS and her

Greatest Fear, but I couldn't relate to her . . . or so I thought. See, I've always been a "brave" person—even living overseas and raising four children in Siberia. I looked at Izzy and thought she was weak.

Until I started rooting around my past. I went back to a time when I also was struggling to leave my home. I wasn't so much afraid to leave, as I was overwhelmed. When I was in Russia, I had four children under the age of five, some so young I had to carry two of them when we left the house. We lived in a high-rise on the ninth floor. We didn't have a phone. We didn't have Internet. We didn't have running water. I didn't have a car. And we had to walk two blocks to the little grocery kiosk. There were times when my husband would be gone for two or three days, and we'd have nothing but saltines and peanut butter in the cupboard. I'd stare at the empty shelves, wanting to conjure up anything to eat. I would think, *I don't know how I'm going to leave the house to buy food.* I wasn't afraid, but I did feel trapped, and that was enough for me to relate to Izzy. I could point to those memories and say, "Yes, this is what it feels like to be trapped in your home."

From that emotion I was able to create a scene where Izzy actually *was* out of food and she had to go to the store, and I was able to accurately portray her struggle.

If your character's DMS is something you can relate to, something you can pull from your own life, you'll create authentic situations and emotions as you build that character's story. Make sure you pick a Greatest Fear you can wrap your brain or emotions around. However, the beauty of the DMS is that you can pick whatever Greatest Fear you want. So choose wisely.

Two Powerful Uses for the Greatest Fear

The Greatest Fear is used in two powerful ways in your story:

First, you'll be working toward making that Greatest Fear come true by recreating it in the Black Moment Event. The Black Moment Event is at the end of your story. It is when your hero believes that everything is lost, and his Greatest Fear has come true. This gives you plotting fodder! Using the Greatest Fear as a template, you'll brainstorm an event or situation that resurrects this fear in a tangible, believable way. You don't have to set the Black Moment Event in cement, but in the plotting stage you can conjure up a number of fantastic ideas to help in the formation of your plot.

Second, the Greatest Fear adds both motivation and behavior to your character right from the first page. People are wired to avoid the things that are going to hurt us, especially our deepest fears. So as your character walks on the page, he's already going to be making decisions that will protect him and keep him from getting into that dark place.

Izzy, my character from *My Foolish Heart*, wants to never leave her house. So she arranged her life so she'd never have to leave. She knows all the delivery numbers by memory, pays someone to deliver groceries, and has a work-at-home job.

Owen's Greatest Fear is hurting someone he cares about, again. He's probably not going to get into a relationship, right? He's going to hold people at a distance. Immediately we see the kind of person he is as he walks onto the page, and even if we don't know his exact fear, we will glimpse a hint of it in his behavior. This will then raise the curiosity of the reader!

The Greatest Fear is the single most powerful ingredient you can pull from the DMS. It helps you build motivation, behavior, and the essential Black Moment Event that builds the external climax and sets up the Character Change. But it is only one ingredient of your Character Change plot. If you want to create a powerful Internal Journey, you need to dig around the DMS and uncover the Lie your character believes.

The Lie

The Secret Sauce of Character Change

As we've discussed, the inner journey is the point of your character's journey. Yes, your character will solve the plot problem, but at the core of your story your character is overcoming a fear, dying to his old self, and transforming. And the root of the transformation is the Lie he believes.

Everybody walks around with lies they believe. I am a Christian. I believe that God is about breaking us free of our lies with truth. But this is not just a Christian thought—even secular books and movies use this premise.

Let's take a deeper look at this Lie Journey.

Does my hero have to believe a Lie?

I sometimes get asked this question when I'm working with clients in a My Book Therapy session. (My Book Therapy is the writing and coaching community I started.) Clients have done so much work creating a character, trying to figure out who he is, and "What Lie does your character believe" just seems like another mindless question.

It's not. As you've seen, I build my characters on just a few key questions, the most important ones that comprise our lives. The Lie a character believes is one of these essential questions that threads throughout the entire book. Without the Lie, you don't know what the Truth you're aiming for is. Without the Lie, you don't know what your character believes, what his view on the world is, or even how to build his everyday choices.

Once again using Owen Christiansen as our example, the Lie that Owen could believe is that he will never be forgiven. There's no way to repair the damage that he's done. This Lie then determines everything he does. He doesn't go home, he doesn't repair relationships, and in many ways, he doesn't even value his life.

Let's say you're creating a character who was a special ops soldier turned park ranger. What if his DMS was that his best friend died, and he could have saved him? His Lie might be: *I'm guilty of my friend's death. I can never be forgiven.* He's ashamed and hiding from his guilt and pain. As we open the story, he is figuratively and literally hiding out in the woods.

If you're writing an inspirational novel, you can juxtapose this with the Truth found in Lamentations 3:21 that God gives us second chances.

One of my favorite Lie journeys is found in the movie *The Patriot*. Benjamin Martin, the main character, has a deeply embedded Lie because of his DMS. In his DMS, he was involved in a brutal massacre of an Indian village during the French-American War. (By the way, the filmmakers correctly drop hints about this in the first act and reveal the story in Act 2.) Now his Greatest Fear is that the sins of his past are so great that he will never escape them and that they will come back to haunt him, which they do in the death of his son. To bring that home, Martin's Greatest Fear is that this haunting will include the loss of his children and even the fear that his sons will become like him.

The Lie he believes is that there is no honor in war. Thus, when his sons are killed—first Thomas (confirming the Lie) and then Gabriel (when out of revenge, Grabriel attacks his wife's killer and is murdered)—Benjamin's Greatest Fear comes true and the Lie feels real.

This is the composition of the Black Moment: an event, then *the effect* of that event. In other words, the Greatest Fear coming true and the Lie feeling true.

This is also the setup for your character's Epiphany, or Truth, and thus, his Character Change moment. Now we have the ingredients of the Black Moment, that pivotal, essential element of our character's journey.

Next, we need to take a look at the emotional repercussions of the DMS: our character's Wound.

Our Wounds Define Us

The Wound

Every specific, relatable, poignant DMS cause deep emotional wounds. The Wound is the emotional damage wrought by the DMS. It's that gaping, raw, open place that is the emotional reaction to the event.

The Wound for Owen after his family fight is rejection. He thinks, "My family sided with Casper, not with me. I've been rejected. No one is on my side."

The Wound is important because it's the emotional reaction to the DMS. Your character will protect his Wound, and you, as the author, will use it to cause damage to your character.

Wounds, and the healing of them, are also essential tools. If you're writing a romance, you'll use the characters' Wounds to cause the essential breakup. Similarly, the Wounds are then healed by the hero and heroine. In other genres, your character's Wound can be healed by someone significant, e.g., you might have a mother heal the Wound of a daughter or a friend heal the Wound of your character. The Wound is also used to detour a hero from his goal, especially near the end of the story. Most importantly, the ending will provide healing for the Wound in a visible way. The Wound provides an author with a technique to show how your character has changed.

One of my favorite Wound-healing moments is in *While You Were Sleeping*. The heroine, Lucy, has always wanted to travel. However, she's been unable to do this because of her father's death. The hero, Jack, first hints that he *can* heal her Wound by giving her a snow globe with a scene of Florence. Then, for their honeymoon, he gives her a stamp in her passport. In essence, he's giving her the world and heals her Wound.

The Wound also directs your character's choices and behavior. A character will protect himself from getting hurt again, and thus, as your character walks onto the page, you'll see him protecting himself from further wounding through his actions and choices. The Wound provides powerful motivation for your character's dialogue as he interacts with other characters.

But first, you must discover the Wound that needs to be healed. This is found by asking three questions:

- What emotional hurt did the DMS cause?

- What longing does your character have that is specific to this moment?

- What small gesture would help ease the pain of this Wound?

Owen's Wound is rejection and especially feeling left out of the family. When his family not only accepts him back but also rallies around him in his darkest hour, they heal his Wound. When the girl he loves leads this charge, the heroine also heals this Wound.

Discovering the character's Wound and healing it also adds the emotional layer to your character's final happy ending.

But before your hero can have that happy ending, he must complete his Character Change Journey and overcome his Final Battle. In order to see that internal change, we look at your character's Flaw.

The Flaw

The Flaw: The External Expression of the Greatest Fear

The DMS is the key for pulling out the Greatest Fear, Lie, and Wound . . . but we also need to discover your character's Flaw if we want to complete his Character Change Journey.

Why is it important to have a Flaw for your character?

If you're looking for a litmus test to show that your character has changed by the end of the story, we look at his Flaw. The Flaw is the glue that binds together the external plot and the internal plot of the Lie journey.

How? Flaws often come from our greatest fears, as protective mechanisms to prevent our greatest fears from occurring. We create these behaviors, which are actually flaws, to keep us safe.

Owen's Flaw stems from his fear of getting hurt and having his family abandon him. So he reasons, "I'm not going to get into relationships. I'm going to be very cold with people because I don't want to hurt someone again, and I don't want to be hurt again."

Women often have flaws based on their worries. They look ahead and think, "Oh, I don't want that to happen so I'm going to make sure it doesn't. I'm going to act in a certain way to prevent my perceived fear from becoming reality."

For women, many of our fears stem from our children or our marriages. We hear the story of a friend and her horrific divorce after the husband's affair, so we start to get nervous and start wondering if it could happen to us. The next thing we know, we're reading hubby's text messages, snooping, and acting in a crazy, suspicious, flawed way.

Or a woman might be overprotective or hovering, or the fear that someone will fail us can cause us to be demanding or exacting. All these flaws are based on perceived fears.

On the flip side, men often have flaws based on something that has already happened in their past that they fear repeating. They resolve to never repeat their mistakes, so they take action to avoid the situation they fear. They reason, "I was rejected, so I'm not going to get into a relationship again. I was blamed, so I'm not going to give advice again."

To discover your character's Flaw, look at your character's Greatest Fear and ask: *How is that expressed in a Flaw?*

Let's take a look again at *The Patriot*. Benjamin Martin has a clear Flaw at the beginning of the movie. He won't fight. Why? He fears dying and not providing for his family. Or his sons following him into war. Or losing his family. All reasonable fears based on his past relationship with war and his fear that the sins of his past will return to haunt him.

In Owen Christiansen's recent DMS, he lost—even destroyed—the relationship with his brother. His Greatest Fear is that he is going to wreck his relationships—so he's been keeping all his relationships at a shallow level for the past couple of years . . . until he meets a girl who gets to know him and seems to like him. In fact, she sees past his darkness. So what does he do? Knowing that this just might be his one and only chance, he's suddenly impulsive—

grabbing onto the relationship before it can get away. He has to learn to be brave and let people love him on their own, to choose him, which ultimately will heal his Wound.

In your hero's Character Change Journey, his Flaw is healed after the Epiphany when the character realizes the Truth, is set free from the Lie, overcomes his Greatest Fear, and then acts in a changed way, healed from the Flaw, as a New Man (or Woman!).

It's at this point that your character does something at the end of the book he couldn't at the beginning because he's been changed. It's this external act that reveals the internal change.

This key moment is the cherry on top of your story, the ultimate moment in the climax where the hero finally achieves triumph. It's what your reader has been waiting for.

See, that wasn't so hard, was it?

The SEQ has now given us the character's identity, his DMS, the Greatest Fear, the Lie, the Wound, and the Flaw—all of which help us build the external plot points and inner journey of our character.

However, we still need to know what our character Wants to help us build the compelling dilemma that drives your character through the plot of the story.

What does your character Want?

So far, the SEQ has helped us discover our character's:

- Identity

- Dark Moment Story (DMS)

- Greatest Fear (our external conflict),

- Lie (internal conflict)

- Wound

- Flaw (the emotional expression of our Greatest Fear and Wound).

All these elements work together to build the driving force or motivation for what our character wants.

The Want is the culmination of these elements—it's something deep inside your character that motivates and reinforces your character's Goal or Noble Quest—or the external plot of the story. In other words, the Want is the force inside him that propels him to pursue the quest upon which he's been called, as a result of the Inciting Incident.

Let's use Owen again as an example. His DMS was losing his relationship with his family. What does he want? A relationship with his family . . . or even just *a* family.

Because Owen is a person who wants to return home and yet can't, he's never really settled down anywhere else. He's a transient worker. Why? Because his Greatest Desire is to return home and he believes that if he settles down he'd be saying, "I'm never going home." So for him, his Want is expressed in taking part-time jobs.

The Want propels every choice, every piece of dialogue, every action. Even if the character doesn't talk about it, it's inside him and it's part of his motivation. Most importantly, that Want is present from the first moment he's on the page. In other words, he walks on to the page fully formed because he's already been acting in his Want his whole life.

But the Want is not the Noble Quest, nor is it your character's goal. The Want is internal. The Noble Quest, or character goal, is external. (Only with strong external goals can you create great on-the-page conflict.) **Restated, the goal is the external representation of what he wants.**

I want to add a caveat here. When your character first enters the story, if the Inciting Incident hasn't yet occurred, he will still have a goal, just one that is unaffected by the Noble Quest, that he will receive after the Inciting Incident. That goal will drive his actions in the first scene, even if it is not a monumental goal.

So how does this work in a novel? Your character walks onto the page with that Want embedded inside him, but your character is acting in what is called his "normal life." He has a goal for his current situation, a goal for that first scene. If the Inciting Incident has already occurred, then that goal is possibly his Noble Quest. If not, then the Inciting Incident ignites the Noble Quest, and the Want solidifies that into the story goal.

Some stories start out with the character's goal as the driving force, and the Inciting Incident sticks a monkey wrench into that goal. In this case, when you're deciding your character's goal, you start with the Want. Then ask the SMART question: *How is this expressed in something Specific, Measurable, Achievable, Realistic, and Timely?* When the Inciting Incident occurs, the goal is adjusted to fit the Noble Quest.

As Owen's story opens, his Want is to go home. But he has no reason beyond his desire to take any actionable steps. His goal is simply: "I'm going to catch fish, make money, and figure out what I'm going to do next." That's how he starts the first scene.

Shortly after the book opens, however, a shipmate gets thrown overboard into the Bering Sea, and Owen actually jumps in after her (because he's a real hero). His goal first is to save her, then, when they get on a life raft, his goal becomes to live through this ordeal.

This Inciting Incident solidifies his resolve to return home. Therefore, when, as a result of him being thrown into the sea, Owen's brother arrives and gives him an ultimatum about returning home, Owen agrees. The plot thickens when Owen discovers that his brother is wanted for a crime he didn't commit. Now, Owen's goal has changed and becomes SMART: to clear his brother's name and to restore his own place in the family—all fueled by his original Want.

We sometimes use the words "Secret Desire" in place of Want as we build the character motivation. It has more of an emotional element to it in the sense that the Secret Desire is more specific, more poignant. "I want to be restored to my family" is a stronger desire than "I want to be a part of a family." Because of this Secret Desire, when Owen's captain, whom he is attracted to but has kept his distance from, goes overboard, he then reacts almost as a family member and goes in after her. Although he still has his wounds, his Secret Desire and natural heroism take over to push him forward into the decision.

Once you have a goal, then you can insert obstacles into your story and begin to cause tension.

How do you find that Want or Secret Desire?

The Want/Secret Desire is a product of both the DMS and your character's Greatest Dream.

The DMS can build the Want by giving your character a desire for justice or restoration, something to fix.

If you're having trouble finding the Want/Secret Desire, ask your character what his Happiest Moment of the Past was. Just like drilling down to find the DMS, go back to your character interview and ask your character to tell you a story—specific, poignant, relatable—about one of his happiest memories.

You'll use this in two ways:

- First, ask your character why this moment was his happiest, and you'll find the ingredients for his Secret Desire/Greatest Dream.

For example, Owen's Happiest Moment was simply raking the leaves with his brothers and jumping in them in the autumn. Why? Because there was nothing between them but friendly, brotherly competition, and he felt as if he belonged, that he wasn't different from them, and that they liked him. Because he feels estranged from them, reconciling to return to this moment feels like a great dream. (Of course, this is exactly what we give him in the end.)

- Second, you'll use this story as another way to connect your readers to your character when Owen shares this vignette with another person on the page. We'll see his true heart, and he'll become even more likeable.

The Want/Secret Desire is the fuel behind the Noble Quest/Goal. Pull it from your DMS and your Happiest Moment Story and you'll have the right ingredients to motivate your character forward into the story. You'll also be able to create external conflict by finding obstacles to those goals.

But first, let's find that inner conflict. We do that by causing inner dissonance, or discovering Competing Values.

The Anguish of Competing Values

The Inner Conflict

Once you discover your character's Want—and can then create powerful Goals—you have the means to start adding conflict. Great external conflict is created when a character desires something (Want), establishes a Goal, and then runs up against an obstacle. When you have something to lose, or stakes, tension is created as the character tries to overcome the obstacle.

So the Want+Goal combination helps you discover external obstacles.

But we also need internal obstacles for a character to create inner dissonance. Inner dissonance results when our character wants two equally worthy things.

We create internal obstacles by *pitting our values against each other.* Everybody has values, things that they care about, things that they believe in, things that drive them. Our values push us through positive decisions and help us cope with difficult situations. But when they are in dissonance, we have internal conflict.

How Competing Values Work

During my son's senior year and my daughter's sophomore year of high school, I had a moment of Competing Values.

Every year I held the prom party in town. (It is a very small town.) This particular year, I realized I had scheduled a teaching event in Colorado at the same time I'd scheduled the prom party. I thought, "I can't do this. This is not going to work." I was having a value conflict because I want to be a great teacher and keep my commitments. When I'm with students, I'm 100 percent invested.

But I also want to be a great mom. When I'm a mom I'm 100 percent there, and I'm going to throw the best party in town for my kids. My values were in conflict because I couldn't be in two places at the same time.

These values not only caused conflict, but they also drove my decisions. I ended up calling the conference director and asking her to move all my classes to Thursday and Friday. (Prom was on Saturday night.) Saturday morning I got up at 3:00 a.m. I drove from the mountains of Colorado down to Denver, three hours away. I got on a plane, flew to Minneapolis, got on another plane, and flew to Duluth. Then I got in my car and drove three hours up the shore to our tiny hometown. I pulled in at 4:00 p.m. I had already enlisted an army of moms to help me, given them assignments, and we met at the party just in time. But my great quest was fueled by my dual values.

Now it would have been even better—not more convenient, but a better story—if I had gotten to Minneapolis and the plane wouldn't start or there was blizzard, which could happen in May in Minnesota. Or if I had to hitchhike and get in the car with strangers and we drove to Duluth and from there had to find a dog sled . . .

The point is, Competing Values can help you create great internal conflict. Stories stick with us when they make a reader have to choose between two equally worthy values.

Sophie's Choice? Hello? Or *Sommersby?* Competing Values add poignant, powerful, emotional moments to a story.

If you're writing a suspense, it might be a choice between saving the girl or getting the bad guy. Or the hero choosing to sacrifice himself or fighting his way to freedom. You'll use Competing Values all the way through the story, but having them emerge during the climax is especially powerful.

How do you discover your character's Competing Values?

Use the DMS! Usually we value what we really want or something that has saved us.

What are Owen's values? Family, yes, but we also need another value—preferably an opposite value—in order to cause inner dissonance. As we evaluate Owen, a former hockey player, we can also see that he's always wanted to be a superstar. He wants that feeling of "I've accomplished something. I've done something great," but instead, he's a failure in his own eyes. This could probably be boiled down to a value of success or victory.

Now that we have these two values, at a climactic moment he will have to choose between victory or his family. He'll have to choose to sacrifice one to save the other (and he does!).

Now that we've used the SEQ to build our character, we need to understand how to use these essential pieces. The good news is that they fit neatly into a story grid or external story structure. We'll take a look at how you can build one of those next.

Section Three
Using the SEQ to Plot Your Story

External Story Structure: The LINDY HOP

It's one thing to build a powerful character—but if you can't show his Character Change through a compelling external plot, then he is simply a layered character with nowhere to go. The beauty of the SEQ is that it provides you with all the elements you need to put your story together at a high level.

First, however, we need to take a look at the external structure of your story. The LINDY HOP is an acronym that I came up with years ago at My Book Therapy to explain the external journey of your character's story. We call it the LINDY HOP because I love dancing and also because it's this really nifty acronym that helps us put it all together. Here it is:

L — Life
I — Inciting Incident
N — Noble Quest
DY — Disappointments/ Y-in-the-road
H — Help
O — Overhaul
P — Perfect Ending

For the purpose of this section, we'll separate the story or the external plot into three acts because that's the standard. But we all know that Act 2 is actually two parts, right? Usually, Act 1 is about 15 percent of your story, Act 3 is about 15 to 20 percent of your story, and Act 2 is everything in the middle.

Act 1, the Bio Sets Up the Story

L stands for Life. Life is that normal world where your character finds himself as your readers enter the story. The characters are already fully formed. They have their Lies, their Wounds, their Greatest Fears. They have their Goals, their Wants, their Competing Values, and their Flaws as they walk onto the page. And this is the world where your character normally lives.

If you were doing a weight-loss journey, this would be your *before* picture. We're going to see a snapshot of who your character is as he interacts with people and he goes about his daily life. The Life part helps the readers meet your character in his current state so that at the end, they can take a look again and think, "Wow! What a change." If we don't have those "before" snapshots, then it's difficult to see the change that your character goes through.

After Life, your character experiences his **Inciting Incident** where something *happens*. The something that happens can be either big or small, but it's a blip in his everyday world. The result of the Inciting Incident is that he has to make a choice about whether he's going to go forward or backward.

Just a note: The Inciting Incident does not have to happen on page one. You might start your story with the Inciting Incident having already happened, with your character reacting to that situation, and returning to Life as he tries to figure out what to do. Only then does he go forward on his **Noble Quest**.

Or you might have the Inciting Incident happen right as the story opens, and now your character has to react to it and then go on his Noble Quest.

Or you might start with a nice long Life scene and hint at the Inciting Incident that happens in a later scene.

Where the Inciting Incident occurs depends on the pacing and flow of your story—and to some extent, your genre. But at some point in Act 1 you need to have the Inciting Incident.

The Inciting Incident can be a negative event that your character then tries to fix throughout the rest of the story. Or it could be a positive event. Maybe he wins the lottery. He thinks, "Oh this is awesome. I won, and I'll make sure that we always have money now." So his Noble Quest is to hold onto the cash.

Regardless of when your Inciting Incident happens, the result is an invitation to go on a journey. This journey is going to be what he does for the rest of the book.

Once the Inciting Incident occurs, we need a reaction to it and an invitation to go on the Noble Quest. It might not look like an "invitation," but rather a necessity. However, everyone has a choice, and thus your character must have a **Great Debate**, weighing the pros and cons, then choosing to go on the journey. The Great Debate causes the character to ask: *Should I go or should I stay? Should I go on this journey or not?*

If you don't have a Great Debate that happens between the Inciting Incident and the Noble Quest and your characters simply launch out on their journey without thinking about it, it's very likely you will have readers who question the journey. Worse, they won't agree with it and will put the story down. Make your character consider all the options—the negative consequences and the stakes (what could happen if he doesn't take the journey)—then use his Values and Secret Desire to push him onto the Noble Quest. By the way, he might refuse to go on the journey, which then causes him to revisit the effect of the Inciting Incident or even have yet another "invitation," which he then accepts.

Now, let's say your character's Inciting Incident occurs when he arrives home and finds his house is on fire and his dog trapped inside. He doesn't think, "Oh, should I go in the house or not?" He acts on instinct and races into the house to rescue the dog. That's simply a *reaction* to the Inciting Incident. He is not on his Noble Quest at that point.

Now he comes out and a fireman says, "We suspect arson." Maybe your hero is a fireman and responds with, "I'm going to find out who did this." He's going to have a Great Debate at this point to figure out what he should do next on his journey.

A lot of times people think, "Because my character reacted to the Inciting Incident, he is now on his journey." Not necessarily. He can react and still have a Great Debate after that before he starts on the major journey of the story.

Without Life, the Inciting Incident, a Great Debate, and the Noble Quest, we don't have a full understanding of who your character is, why the Noble Quest is important, or even a hint of what he might learn. It's important to keep in mind that while the story is about the external things that your character does, it's also about the internal Character Change. So it's very important that we spend some time meeting your character and seeing his Life, or the "before" shot, even if you have an Inciting Incident that happens right away or before the story opens.

That's Act 1.

Act 2 now commences all the fun and games that happen in the middle of the book

The point of Act 2 is to bring your character along the journey that causes character growth—and this is caused by obstacles, or what we call Disappointments.

During Act 2, we're going to feed the character lies and truth. We're going to test his character and mettle. More importantly, we're going to make things worse and heighten the stakes of the story.

And every time something happens to your character, he'll find himself in a position where he has to make a choice. He's going to try to figure out, "What should I do? Should I go this way or a different way?" The choices he makes will be based on his values. This is where you can use your Competing Values. He might be driven by one value in one situation and a different one in the next.

Every choice will cause him to make a turn in the journey, a **"Y" in the road**.

The Ys in the road represent the decisions that the hero makes after every major conflict. Again, every decision he makes is based on his values, his goals, his motivations, his fears (making sure he doesn't go and repeat his past), his flaws, and what's at stake in the story. Every decision for your character is different, just like it is for you.

The key for you as an author is to make sure that your readers agree with every decision that your character makes. Even if they don't agree with the overall decision per se, they believe that each decision is one that the character *might make* in that moment. It must make sense given his current situation, his choices, his overall goals, his motivations, and his values.

Your job is to build up the motivation and all these internal elements so that when he makes the decision to run into the building to save the dog, the reader says, "*Yes, he's a fireman. The fire isn't unbearable yet. He knows exactly where the dog is. And this is his last chance to do it. So run, fireman hero, into the house and save the dog!*"

Act 2 follows these Disappointments and Ys in the road until the character gets to the bridge between Act 2 and Act 3, otherwise known as the Black Moment. In the LINDY HOP, we call it **Help**. Remember, the substance of your Black Moment is your character's Greatest Fear coming true (Event) and the Lie that he believes feeling real (Effect).

Act 3 is the plot climax and character change finale

Act 3 is also where your character receives his *Aha!*, Epiphany moment of truth that will set him free. Now your character is changed, his Flaw is healed, and he's a new man, armed with new beliefs, strengths, and courage to face the climatic ending. This is the **Overhaul**.

Now we end the story then with the **Perfect Ending**. The perfect ending is a combination of the character's Greatest Dream coming true and the Wound being healed.

See how much of this external story structure (and quite a bit of the internal structure) you've already plotted. The story is practically half written!

Let's Sum Up:

- Once upon a time **(Life)**

- Something out of the ordinary happens **(Inciting Incident)**

- Causing the protagonist to seek something **(Noble Quest)**

- But things don't go as expected **(Disappointments)**

- Forcing the protagonist to make a difficult decision **(Ys in the road)**

- Which has dark consequences **(Help!)**

- The result of which is an *Aha!* Moment to make him a new person **(Overhaul)**

- And they all lived happily ever after **(Perfect Ending)**

There you have the basics of story structure. Now let's add the ingredients of our Story Equation!

Internal Plot/Lie Journey

The power of the Lie

What Lies do you believe? How do they control your life? I'll bet as you've been reading this book, you've been thinking through your own life, your own Dark Moments, and how they've conspired to mold you into the person you are today.

Past events imprison you in Lies you believe, with Fears, and Flaws. See, our imaginary characters are not so different from us.

The goal of our character's journey is to set him free from the Lie he believes and transform him into a New Man.

What does that inner journey look like? Let's start with a roadmap:

Step One: Spiritual Darkness —The Lie He Believes

We've already covered the DMS and how it is key in discovering your character's Lie. Now, to begin the journey, try to boil down your character's inner need in one sentence. What Truth does he need to embrace in order to be set free?

In my book *Happily Ever After*, my heroine, Mona, needed to trust God and forgive herself (and accept God's forgiveness). My hero, Joe, needed to forgive his father.

In Francine River's book *Redeeming Love*, Angel needed to accept God's unconditional love and forgiveness, and then see Hosea as God's instrument to love her.

Establish the Lie and determine the Truth that will set your character free. Knowing this will help you figure out where you're going, what truthlets to drop, and how to build the Epiphany moment.

Step Two: Confirmation of the Lie —Proof

Raise your hand if you believe you have no redeeming qualities. That's craziness! See, we all stand outside each other's Lies and think: *How can they think that way? Doesn't she know how beautiful she is? Talented? Smart? No, we don't, and our character doesn't either.* The problem is the reader stands on the sidelines and doesn't understand how the character can believe that Lie.

So you as the author need to prove it to the reader. You do this by showing a moment that confirms the Lie for the reader. You need to convince the reader that the character has a reason to believe that his Lie is real.

Another way to look at it is to again convince the hero that his Lie is true. You want to do something that will cement him into this Lie and, of course, it needs to be something that only pushes him deeper into trouble.

In *Nothing but Trouble*, PJ Sugar, my heroine, believes that she can do no right and that God isn't on her side. In fact, she believes that she's a sort of misfit, and that He has no use for her, even though she is saved. And in the first part of the book, the reader sees this as true. Her pastor boyfriend rejects her, her nephew, whom she is supposed to take care of, hates her, and when she tries to help a friend in trouble, it only backfires on her. She is convinced that she is *nothing but trouble*.

We've already touched on *The Patriot* and Benjamin Martin's tell-tale piece of dialogue: *"I have long feared that the sins of my past would come back to revisit me."* But we don't believe it . . . until we see it. The confirmation of the Lie occurs after Thomas is killed and our hero leads his two other sons to ambush the Redcoats and save his son Gabriel. His words—his sins, the fact he is a monster, and that there is no honor in war—are confirmed in the Dark Moment when his grief boils over and he grotesquely attacks the already deceased soldier in the riverbed.

It's a long and gruesome scene and cements in the viewer's mind the fact that yes, there is no honor in war, and Martin is truly a brutal man, despite the tenderness with which he cares for his children.

We believe his Lie. Or, more importantly, we understand how he could believe it. Set up the Lie, and then prove it to the hero/heroine.

Step Three: The Voice of Truth

In every book, just like in life, secondary characters stand outside the Lie. It's essential for the character to interact with someone who sees the Truth and can declare it—either directly, in actions, or in some subtexted speech to the hero/heroine. These "truth tellers" drop "truthlets," or pieces of truth, to the main character that will linger and do their job during the finale of the book.

In *The Patriot*, because of his past, Benjamin Martin believes that being "bloodthirsty" is the only way to win the war. Gabriel, his son, represents the Voice of Truth. Gabriel believes there is honor in war. This is shown in numerous ways, most notably in the difference between the men they recruit. Benjamin heads to a bar and signs up the ruffians who are drinking. Gabriel heads to a church and delivers a rousing speech that then galvanizes the men to action.

It is notable that at the end of the movie, it is the men from church who have stayed the course, through the brutal way, and have returned to help Benjamin Martin rebuild his house—showing that men of honor can fight war.

Truthlets are also dropped by Gabriel in a conversation he has with his father. Benjamin Martin is melting down the chess pieces of his deceased son's army men, and Gabriel watches him, finally saying, "If you're here only for revenge, you're doing a disservice to Thomas, as well as yourself."

He implants the idea that they are there for a higher purpose. It's not about being bloodthirsty, but being men of honor. Martin struggles to see the difference . . . because he wasn't a man of honor before . . . and he isn't sure he can be one now.

The truthlets can be dropped throughout the entire book, but primarily in Act 2. Ask: *Who is the Voice of Truth in your story, and in a way that isn't preaching, what can he or she say that drops a crumb of Truth that will later nourish that Epiphany?*

Step Four: The Realization of the Lie and the Testing of the Truth

At some point, your hero has to see that he's been living in the Lie and that he *can* change. He has to see there is another way—if only he can embrace the Truth. He might even try it.

This usually happens in Act 2B, after the midpoint. In *The Patriot*, Benjamin's band attacks a Redcoat caravan. There are a number of soldiers who want to surrender, but Benjamin's men kill them. Gabriel, the Voice of Truth, is horrified, and seeing his horror, Benjamin decides to try it Gabriel's way. He declares that they will give mercy to all the other captured soldiers in the future. And then he "tests the water" by saving the two Great Danes belonging to an English officer. Later on, those Great Danes come to love Benjamin and are loyal to him, a metaphorical Truth that when he does right, he will earn others' esteem and be the man he wants to be.

This is not the Epiphany moment but rather, a testing of the Truth that affords a taste of Victory, of Character Change, and Truth that allows him to embrace it fully in Act 3.

How can your character embrace a part of this Truth—enough to taste some success before the fall?

Step Five: Black Moment

We've talked about the Black Moment Event, the external events that lead to the Black Moment Effect. During the Black Moment Effect, the Lie rears its ugly head, and the hero is caught in the darkness. Again, this occurs right before the Epiphany. In this moment he realizes that, although he's tried to escape on his own, the Lie has imprisoned him and is pulling him back in.

This is a brutally sad scene in *The Patriot.* Just before the Black Moment Event, the viewer is set up when Benjamin finally telling his son what his Greatest Fear is: "When I went to war, it changed me. And I didn't want that to happen to you."

Gabriel responds by saying, "Don't worry, Father, you taught me well." However, shortly thereafter, Gabriel's wife is tragically killed, and Gabriel is grief-stricken and filled with vengeance. In that moment, Gabriel turns into a man bent on revenge, chases after the murderer (the same soldier who killed his brother), and is killed in the ensuing battle.

Benjamin is devastated. His worst fears have happened: He has lost his son, in part because of his own actions. In that moment he returns to the belief that, although he's tried to fight honorably, the sins of his past have caught up to him. He has lost his children, and if he can't fight for revenge, then he's lost his reason for fighting.

The Black Moment Effect is when the Lie seems bigger than life and is inescapable.

Step Six: The Aha! The Truth That Sets Them Free

And now it's time for Truth to set our hero free. It's wonderful if it is delivered in a metaphorical moment, but it also works through another Voice of Truth.

After Gabriel's death, Benjamin's fellow soldier General Lee comes to Benjamin and tries to console him. He tells Benjamin that his losses matter to everyone and that he has other children to fight for.

Lee says, "Nothing will replace your sons, but if you come with us, you can justify their sacrifice."

Benjamin says nothing, and we think he hasn't heard him. But great change occurs, first inside, and then it is revealed through action. As the militia and Continental army are leaving and Benjamin looks like he's deserting, he sees a flag that Gabriel had been mending throughout the movie. It's a metaphor for the vision and honor of the fight. In that moment, Benjamin Martin realizes that there are some causes worth fighting for, and that he can fight for honor rather than revenge.

But the story isn't over quite yet. We'll talk about the last step when we discuss the Character Change Journey.

Mapping out the spiritual journey can be as extensive or as minimal as you want. I like to define the six steps that I've just outlined and let the story and characterization take it from there.

One of the tricks that really helps me is to post the Lie and the Truth on my computer as I write so I know where I'm going. Maybe you want to plot each point and write out a long theological statement for every leg of the journey. That's fine too—whatever helps you stay on track and ends with your hero at his destination: the Truth that sets him free.

Putting it all together into a Plot

Now it's time to utilize your SEQ to brainstorm your plot.

Life

As we start the story, you'll grab the Want, the Lie, the Fear, and maybe even your character's Flaw. Why? Because these are the components of your character: who he is, what he wants, why he wants it, and what Lie he believes. And remember, our fears are represented in our flaws. He should be walking on to the page with those flaws.

We also need to hint at his Want.

Inciting Incident

Even though we have something that happens, we'll need to follow it up with the Great Debate, then the Noble Quest. We'll get the elements of the Great Debate from his Want and his Competing Values. However, we'll also add in a hint of his Greatest Fear.

We'll also add in the Goals to help us build the Noble Quest and hint at a few of the known obstacles, so we know what we're up against.

Now we have everything we need for Act 1. Of course that's not everything you're going to put in Act 1. You're going to add in interactions and dialogue with other people and stakes and layers of storyworld. But you've got the basics for now, everything you need to ignite his journey.

Act 2

Act 2 is full of Disappointments, which we get from our character's Flaws, his Goals (so we know what obstacles to add), and Competing Values (pitting them against each other) to create internal obstacles.

We'll also use the Lie and start adding in truthlets (small pieces of Truth) via characters and events.

At this point we're just brainstorming. We're pulling out more situations that we can use to write a story. And if you're an organic writer and don't like to plot, you could brainstorm ideas and just pick from them as you're moving along, choosing those that make sense and relate to your character's growth.

One of the areas I think many organic writers struggle with (and I did, too) is the plethora of fantastic ideas. I know fabulous brainstormers. They think of fantastic, dramatic, wonderful story plots. But sometimes their great ideas have nothing to do with the Character Change Journey. The SEQ, when used in conjunction with brainstorming, helps keep these ideas in line with your story.

In Act 2, you, as the author, need to gather up your obstacles, your flaws, and your truthlets and take a look at what other problems you're going to cause for your character. What I usually do in Act 2 is make a story web. I start with my character in the middle and simply start brainstorming trouble. I look at my character's goals and figure out what obstacles I can throw up to detour him and take him further from his Goal with every step.

Once I've brainstormed these ideas, I line them up and consider how I could make each situation build the tension, raising the stakes of the story internally and externally. Often I take all the big, brilliant pieces, put them on note cards, and just move them around the table to see how they might flow.

The goal is to just generate ideas. The key is to keep these ideas aligned with your SEQ, with character motivation, and values.

Make sure, however, that each solution creates a new, direr situation with more painful choices all the way to the Black Moment Event, or the realization of the Greatest Fear.

This is the end of Act 2.

Help!

This is where you'll use the combination of the Greatest Fear and the Lie to pull together the Character Change and climatic ending. At this point you're just trying to come up with a Black Moment Event that works. We don't have to know all the details, just a big picture view.

The key is, your Black Moment has to be integral to the story, to the character, and to his Greatest Fear to align with the story.

Now you've got your Black Moment Event and Effect. You're ready to plot the Overhaul.

Overhaul

It's time to add in Truth and overcome the Flaw. You'll take a look at the Lie to find the Truth, have him learn something, and suddenly see his Lies and Flaws. This is also where you build in a Character Change moment that has your character doing something at the end that he can't at the beginning. That action shows that he's made the change.

He's ready for his Happily Ever After.

Perfect Ending

A Happily Ever After ending is a combination of the fulfillment of his Greatest Dream (or Secret Desire) and the healing of his wounds.

For example, in Owen's case, remember one of his happiest moments was playing in the leaves with his brothers on a fall day. We use it in the story when he tells the heroine about this memory, revealing that his Greatest Dream is to be reunited with his family.

When he returns, thankfully it is fall. They have a family barbecue on the deck, the brothers playing football, leaves falling from the trees. In that moment Owen's Wound is also healed because his family says, "We're so glad you're back." His Perfect Ending is achieved when I combine some element of his Greatest Dream or Secret Desire with a moment where his Wound is healed.

Obviously at this point, your plot is loose, expandable, and subject to great change. But suddenly, your story seed has transformed into a rough idea from which you can keep brainstorming, digging down into a plot, or even start writing.

But you still need to add a final ingredient before you start honing your plot.

Stakes/Why Should We Care?

Why do we care?

After all this work, if you don't include the final storycrafting ingredient, it's like making chocolate chip cookies without the chocolate chips.

Without this final ingredient, you'll have a nice story . . . that a reader will put down. Because without this ingredient, there's nothing holding the reader to the story. Because every reader is going to ask: **Why does it matter? Why should I spend my time reading this book?**

The Stakes of the story are the answer.

Stakes are those things that drive the story, that make the reader say, *Hey, I'm worried about this character, and I have to know what happens.* The Stakes might not be huge starting out, but by the end of the book, they should be worth all the effort the hero (and the reader) has put in to get there. Stakes connect the big picture plot with the heart of your reader and give the reader something to root for in the story.

Three Kinds of Stakes

There are three kinds of Stakes: Public, Personal, and Private. Each of them is compelling in its own way.

Public Stakes have much to do with public values. For example, during WWII, the public value was very much about protecting our country and banding together to fight the war. So stories about freedom and battle were popular stakes in books and movies, and they still are.

Consider some epic movies of my time: *Star Wars*, the battle for freedom against the Empire. A very World War II feeling to these movies.

How about *The Hunt for Red October*, a movie about saving the world from a Cold War weapon and a Russian attack.

Or even *Independence Day*—saving the world from an alien invasion.

Even a movie like *Erin Brockovich*, which is about saving a town from toxic water and the legal battle for individual rights, is about battle and freedom on a cultural level.

Consider the TV series *24*. The Stakes for every season centered around some national terror that the hero, Jack, had to prevent.

Our culture loves movies about fighting for freedom. The movies playing during a Fourth of July holiday include: *The Patriot, Independence Day, Live free or Die Hard, Pearl Harbor,* and even the Captain America movies. All stories where the Stakes are Public—saving a country or the world from tyranny. The first way to make your story matter is to give it Public Stakes.

Ask yourself: Is the issue in the story pertinent to the public values? Does it touch the heart of all of us? Does it tap into the American Dream?

Ask yourself: What do I fear? What public event do I fear happening? A wildfire burning my home? Being a part of a terrorist bombing while at Disneyland? How about getting a disease while on an airplane, then carrying it home? If you fear it, then others fear it also. And that's where you find your Public Stakes.

However, admittedly, these Public Stakes, while epic, don't always touch the heart of the viewer or the reader. To create more powerful Public Stakes, add in a Personal Stake. Let's take another look at some of those epic movies.

Star Wars, while an epic story about the Empire and the Rebels, is also the story about the redemption of Anakin Skywalker.

And in the series *24*, Jack always had a personal crisis with his family that juxtaposes the public crisis of saving the world.

Consider the movie *Saving Private Ryan*. Despite the backdrop of war, the story is essentially about bringing Private Ryan home to his devastated mother.

The movie *Pearl Harbor* would not be as powerful without the love story.

Even the continuing epic adventures of John McClane in the *Die Hard* movies become more compelling when his wife or daughter is taken hostage by the bad guys.

When you are creating a story with epic Public Stakes, consider making it more compelling by adding a Personal Stake to the story. Can you threaten the family and have the hero fall in love with the one woman who has to possibly give her life to save the day?

The next time you watch an epic, analyze it to see how the writer made the story more compelling by making it personal. What if you took out that personal element? Would you still care about the story?

Public Stakes + Personal Stakes create a powerful combination. This is the second way to make your story matter.

To add in the element of Personal Stakes, ask: What would make my character *not* save the day? What threat could be added to the story on a personal level that would make my character think twice about going into battle? Starting with the end in mind helps you create a story thread that culminates in this decision.

Let's take, for example, the *Titanic* movie. It's epic because of the Public Stakes: 3,000 lives aboard a sinking ship. However, it becomes personal because of the love story between Rose and Jack. What would make our heroine *not* get off a sinking ship? The fact that the man she loves is on board.

This question then leads to so many others: Why can't he get off the ship? What if he was imprisoned on the ship? How would that happen? What if he was arrested? Why? What if it had something to do with the heroine? See, the line of thinking can continue all the way back to the beginning where we discover he's a hustler who won his passage ticket and fell for the wrong girl. Now you've created your personal thread.

The key is that if you use this combination, the Personal Stakes must influence the Public Stakes in some way.

Consider the difference between the Personal Stakes of *Pearl Harbor* and *Independence Day*. The epic Public Stakes of *Independence Day* dictate that the heroes must leave their loved ones behind. The personal layer adds emotion to the story, but doesn't affect the stakes. However, in *Pearl Harbor*, the Personal Stakes are enough to potentially keep one of the heroes from going to battle.

But what if your story has no Public Stakes? What if it is simply about a prairie girl who wants to win a horse race? There's no Public Stakes there.

Who remembers the story of Laura Ingalls Wilder where she rides her horse, Bunny, in a race against bratty Nellie? Why does this story matter? Well, of course, Nellie hates that Laura has a horse and persuades her mother to buy her a fancy horse from Mankato. Laura doesn't have a chance. What's worse, Mrs. Oleson mocks Caroline for being poor and refuses to sell her shoes for her children until she has cash. If Laura wins the race, she'll receive a prize that she can use to pay for the shoes. So she trains Bunny and is ready for the big race when . . . Willie get sick. No one is around to fetch the doctor, so Laura has to make a choice—ride Bunny and risk her being too tired to run the race or let Willie die. What will she do?

This is an example of Private Stakes and how to use them to create a different kind of compelling story. See, behind this story are two Competing Values: family honor and compassion, both of which Laura has in big doses.

Which value will win? When you pit two equally worthy values against each other in a story, you have what we call Private Stakes.

Private Stakes can be found in the root of our values. The things that drive us or the things we long for. Laura longed to show up Nellie and to help her parents. She also knew that to be true to who she was, she had to be compassionate.

When we pit values against each other in a story, it not only makes for great conflict but it touches the heart of your reader in a way that makes the story stick.

All I have to do is mention *Sophie's Choice*. If you've seen the movie, you'll never forget it. How about the movie *Sommersby*?

I'll never forget the day I saw that movie. I sat in the theater and sobbed. (And I'm talking big, sweeping, my-husband-was-embarrassed sobs.) I just couldn't resign myself to the ending. Why? Because my values were assaulted.

In *Sommersby* two men in the Civil War meet in prison, and the key is they look alike. The evil one of the pair dies, but before he dies, he tells the other of his plantation in the South.

The other man, wanting to start a new life, heads to the plantation, impersonating the first man. He doesn't expect to find a wife and to fall in love with her, to have a family with her, and to invest himself in the lives of the town. He gives away a great portion of his land to the emancipated slaves, and seemingly all is good . . . until seven years later, a posse shows up, hunting the deceased man for crimes he committed.

Suddenly, our hero is imprisoned and is going to hang for the crimes of the evil man. Does he tell the truth? If he does, then he will have committed adultery, his child is illegitimate, and most importantly, the land he's given away will no longer belong to the freed slaves. But, if he lies and says he is the man, keeping his family's honor, then he dies.

It's a horrible dilemma, and I was a mess . . . and it was at that moment that I realized that my value of honor was not as strong as my value of happily ever after. I didn't care that the world he created would be destroyed. I just wanted them to be together. It's a powerful story. Why? Not because of any global issue, but because it touched the heart of my own values. It's that kind of story that we never forget.

How do you find the private values of your character? We talked about finding the identity of your character and following that down to his values . . . but here are some simple questions to help you find your character's values:

- What matters most to your character?

- What values drive your character?

- What would your character die for?

To create a compelling story, find two different values, and then ask yourself: In what situation will these values be pitted against each other?

Touch our values, make us think about them, and you'll have created powerful Private Stakes that will move your reader and make your story compelling.

Example: It's a World War II story about a woman who can only choose to save the life of one of her children and the aftermath of that terrible decision (*Sophie's Choice*).

Example: It's the Civil War tale of a man who impersonates another man, only to discover that if he wants to redeem his life, he must lose it (*Sommersby*).

Example: It's a story set during the Revolutionary War about a reluctant patriot who is forced into a war he doesn't want, until he discovers that it's the only way to save his family (*The Patriot*).

Example: A weak man with a bold heart is suddenly given the power to save the world, but the price is the sacrifice of his heart (*Captain America*).

Stakes are the key to every compelling story. Create Public Stakes, a combination of Public and Personal Stakes, or Private Stakes, and you'll have a story your reader can't put down.

Now you're ready to flesh out your story. You've got your SEQ, your loose plot, and you're going to just let the character determine the next steps.

In Section 4, we'll dissect Acts 2A and 2B and dig deeper into the Character Change Journey. (And take some of the muddle out of the middle!)

Section Four
Beginnings, Middles, and End
The Power of the SEQ

The Glue: The Character Change Journey

Every story has two powerful threads: an external plot (we call it the LINDY HOP, right?) and the inner journey, or the DMS. So where does the Character Change Journey fit?

Think of the Character Change Journey as the connective tissue between the inner journey (the Spiritual, or Lie journey) and the external journey (the LINDY HOP). It is both internal and external. For example, the Fear is internal. But the Fear is shown through the behavior of the Flaw. Later, the Fear becomes external when it is realized in an event. This pushes the character into the Black Moment Effect, or the Lie feeling real. The ensuing Epiphany is also internal, although it can be brought about by external elements (actions, dialogue). The Overhaul is portrayed in the healing of the Flaw and then an external action the character takes to show he's been healed and overhauled.

The Character Change Journey touches both the external and internal plot. And, thus, it provides powerful material for our Act 2 A and 2B scenes.

To understand the steps in the journey, I have a grid that helps me move my character from step to step. Think of it as a checklist, just to make sure you've gotten every element of change in the story.

Act 1

The BIO story

- Home
  - Snapshot of GD
  - Lie/Fear/Wound
  - WANT
- Inciting Incident
- Quest

Act 2A

THE CAUSE

(dark moment story)
- Attempt
- Cost
- Reward
- Desire
- Attempt
- MIM

Act 2B

THE FIGHT
(Character changelets)
- Bad
- Badder
- Baddest
  - Taste of Death
  - Taste of Victory
- BMEvent

Act 3

The TRIUMPH
(Leap of Faith/New Man)
- BMEffect
- Overhaul
  - Truth
  - Final Battle
- Perfect Ending

Act 1: The Need to Change

It all starts with a glimpse of what they want.

I finished writing a book this weekend. In between writing and travelling, I haven't had much time to work on my various unfinished remodeling projects, i.e., create a bookshelf in the media room. And paint the family room end wall red.

Yes, *red*. I saw it in a magazine and then at a girlfriend's house, and I thought it would be a striking way to backdrop this incredible piece of artwork I received from a friend. So I sketched out the layout. I got paint samples. I compared them to the picture and my other furniture. I found the right primer. I moved and covered furniture. Last night I primed . . . and this morning . . . I painted. It's drying right now.

But it all started with a sense that my white walls weren't enough. Something was missing. I knew I wanted a pretty room—I just didn't know how to get there.

This is where your character starts as he begins his journey. Something is missing. He doesn't know what it is, but he knows it's not there.

This is what I call a Glimpse of Greatest Dream.

As you open your story, your character is not living his dream. He's "distant" from his Greatest Dream, although he might not even know it. However, as the author, you do (because you've done your SEQ work!) and you need to communicate this, subtly, to your reader. In Act 1 you want the character to do, see, be, or value something that indicates his Greatest Dream.

For example, in *The Lord of the Rings*, Frodo is amazed by his adventurous uncle Bilbo. Frodo loves hearing Bilbo's stories, and is drawn to his bravery. Frodo isn't expressing his desire for adventure or courage—in fact, he doesn't even realize he has it. But we, the readers, see his desire in how he worships his uncle.

Here are some ideas for giving your reader that Glimpse of the Greatest Dream:

- Have your hero do something in which he fails, and have him, or someone else, comment that if he would only do/believe a certain thing, then he might accomplish his task. To which the hero says, "Well, that'll never happen."

- Have your hero, or just your reader, see something that the hero longs for—a happy family, a good job, a hero's welcome. Something that we can later pinpoint as his Greatest Dream.

- Have your hero hear of a story/legend/action that he wishes he could do.

Invitation to Change

After your character glimpses his Greatest Dream—keep it small, maybe even something he doesn't even realize—it's time to offer an Invitation to Change.

The Invitation is that moment very early on when the character is given the opportunity to do something different. To believe something, or value something, or try something. Often he turns it down, and it's that regret that drives him to take the opportunity again.

For example, in *The Patriot*, there is a classic scene in the beginning where Benjamin Martin is talking with his peers who are deciding to go to war with Britain. He says something along the lines of "Principles? I'm a father. I don't have the luxury of principles." The rest of the movie is about him regretting those words.

Sometimes, however, your character immediately accepts the invitation and sees how woefully under-equipped he is. This happens when Bilbo gives Frodo the ring. Frodo reluctantly takes it and has no idea what he's getting himself in for.

Next, you'll give your character an Invitation to Change, something that makes him think about his vacancies, even his Need to Change.

The Need to Change

I could see the problem. Actually, I could smell it. Seeping from my son's tomb-like room. As if, yes, there might be a corpse inside. I stood at the threshold of the doorway and peered in. He lay, a lump under his sheets, the floor of his room riddled with the debris of his teenage-boy existence—old pop cans, bowls of hardened ice cream, decaying socks, his grimy attire from the last week. All marinating in the brew of young-manhood filth.

He needed to clean his room.

I flicked on the light. (Hey, it was 9:00 a.m.) "I think your room needs some attention."

Somewhere beneath the covers, he grunted.

"Seriously, I can't see your floor."

"It's there, or you'd be falling through to the center of the earth."

Oh, so cute. *Ha ha.*

"If you ever want to eat again, I'll see the floor of your room by dinnertime."

"I have to work, I won't be home for dinner."

I flicked off the light. Closed the door. Apparently, my external forces were no longer effective. I had to face the truth. *Change had to come from the inside.*

And only when he recognized the need.

See, a character isn't going to change unless properly motivated. He might see a Glimpse of his Greatest Dream and even be invited by circumstances to change, but without seeing the need, he won't have the strength to tackle the challenges.

The Invitation to Change, whether he accepts it or not, needs to be followed in short order by the Need to Change.

Remember the scene in *The Lord of the Rings* when Frodo and gang are hiding in the woods as the creepy Nazgûl horses are looking for them? Suddenly, for the first time, Frodo realizes the danger they are in. He doesn't fully comprehend it, but he knows it's serious.

He knows he's going to have to do something about it. What, he's not sure, but the need is compelling enough to make him try. (Which will lead us into the second act and his first attempt).

Build into your Character Change an early event or situation that reveals his need to change. It must be a sufficient enough threat that it will force him to confront his demons and fears or beliefs—all those obstacles to change.

These are subtle nuances to your scenes, built into the Life, Inciting Incident, Great Debate, and acceptance of the Noble Quest scenes. The Glimpse of the Greatest Dream might occur in the first scene as a piece of storyworld. The Invitation to Change might also happen in the first scene, when the hero meets the heroine and acts poorly (in his Flaw), and his buddy suggests he could have handled that differently.

Or the Invitation might happen after the Inciting Incident when the hero is debating the Noble Quest. This is also where the Need to Change might appear—for example, if only Benjamin Martin hadn't stayed out of the war, he might not have lost his son Thomas. Or not.

Regardless of when you insert these scenes, they simply add a nuanced motivation to Act 2, where your character is confronted with his Flaw, Lies, and Fears.

Act 2A

Attempt and failure

I love football. Hometown high school, college ball, and pro, in that order. I am a fan of *Friday Night Lights*, every football movie made (well, almost . . . I'm not into the spoofy football movies—it's much too serious a sport for that!), and most of all, football players!

I married a former high-school football player. I like them because when they get hit, they get back up. (Probably why I like bull riders, too.) Does it hurt? Yes. But they shake it off, line up, and try again. They have four downs to get it right.

In Act 1, we set up the elements of Character Change—going through the first elements, the Glimpse of the Greatest Dream, the Invitation to Change, and the Need to Change.

The next and subsequent steps of Character Change are much like the ten-yard run/four downs of a football game.

- Attempt (and Failure)
- Cost Consideration
- Rewards
- Desire
- Attempt and Mini-victory

Let's take a closer look at the football metaphor. The offense has the ball, they need to make their ten yards, and they line up and run the first play. Maybe they drop back for a pass, and our hero, the quarterback (QB), is sacked. Worse, he's injured.

Now the team huddles up. Obviously, the defenders have heard about their amazing passing game, so they'll have to try a different tact. But their superstar fullback is also out of the game (with a mean cold, thanks to this Minnesota weather), so the tailback might not get the blocking he needs for the sweet play. If the QB steps in to block he might get further injured by the rather large senior playing on defense. However, they are on the twenty-yard line and six points down, with a minute left on the board. And if they win this game, they'll go to the state playoffs.

So they run the sweep, and sure enough they get the first down. But the QB is taken out, which opens the door for Act 2B, when our hero, the QB, has to decide if he's really the hero everyone is counting on . . .

Maybe that's too much football, so let's break it down in writer terms.

Attempt and failure

The next stage in the journey is the attempt by the hero to go after the prize, to rescue the fair maiden, or stand up to the bully, or face his fears . . . and his attempts not only fail, but sometimes make everything worse!

Remember when Frodo is enticed to surrender the ring to Galadriel? For the first time, he realizes that he is not quite strong enough to bear this burden. It frightens him, and he's overwhelmed with the task.

Or in *The Patriot*, Benjamin Martin attempts to stay out of the war, only to have his son Thomas killed.

Or in *The Princess Bride*, Buttercup jumps overboard into the sea infested by shrieking eels.

These are external actions, but they affect the character internally. See, your character has charged into the story with great hope and vigor . . .

. . . And been shut down. Now he'll have to huddle up and figure out what to do next. He'll have to consider the cost.

The Cauldron of Cost and Reward

What is it going to cost you? How much are you willing to pay for your freedom? To achieve a goal or dream? To save a loved one? To win love? To achieve your Noble Quest?

These are the questions you, the author, must ask your character as he sits in the dirt, bruised after his Attempt and Failure.

Have you ever been on a diet over Christmas season? I had a Russian friend who was a pilot, and his annual exam arrived right after New Year's Eve. He got his blood drawn and his cholesterol checked. It's a bummer, because in order to keep his pilot's license, he had to pass a certain level.

Which meant he had to diet over Christmas.

Not entirely, but he had to stay away from the rich foods and, of course, wine, which is big in Russia during New Year 's Eve! He stood at the pinnacle of the season, smelled the holiday feast, and lamented his life—or at least the timing of his exam.

But in order to be a pilot, he had to surrender something.

So does your character. Right after he fails his first attempt, he'll have to regroup, take a good look at his weaknesses and vacancies, and realize the truth: If he wants victory, he can't stay the way he is.

Another way to put it: Anything worth fighting for is going to cost something.

Some "considering the cost" moments from my favorite movies:

When Frodo takes off with the boat at the end of *The Fellowship of the Ring* and Samwise nearly dies going after him, Frodo realizes that his quest *will* cost lives and that he has to be brave enough to let that happen.

The Princess Bride: Right after they get through the fire swamp, evil Prince Humperdinck finds them. Buttercup negotiates Westley's release, but surrenders herself to be married to the prince, believing that her man will get killed if she doesn't. She later learns that she must believe that death will not stop true love!

In *You've Got Mail*, we see the cost in the scene where Kathleen and Joe are going to meet in the coffee shop for the first time. Joe sees her and realizes that "ShopGirl" is his nemesis. He'll have to regroup and win her heart online before he can reveal himself. He sacrifices the opportunity in the hopes that something better will transpire.

Give your hero a moment to consider what Character Change will cost him—and have him fear it.

But . . . what is my Reward?

We're not going to fight for something—and sacrifice—if the cost isn't worth it. So as your hero considers the cost, he must also see the reward. How will his life change if he reaches the goal? Is the reward sweet enough?

To dangle that reward in front of him, you, as the author, have to ask: What does your character want? What motivates him to go forward? What's his Secret Desire? What will it cost him to pursue true love? Return to your SEQ for the answers!

In the movie *Titanic*, Rose wants true love, but she also wants freedom from her mother and from societal expectations. When she meets Jack, she discovers the courage to chase her dreams, not her mother's. She sees freedom, tastes it with Jack, and this is her reward.

What about Lucy in *While You Were Sleeping*? She falls in love with Jack, the other brother. But the family she's fallen in love with expects her to marry Peter. If she confesses her feelings, the cost is almost too great. She'll lose this wonderful family because she lied. And she'll lose the man she loves.

But if she takes a chance and confesses that she loves Jack, perhaps she'll get him, the true love she's always wanted.

It's essential that your characters see past the Costs to the Reward. And they have to believe that it's possible. Or at least that it could be. Seeing the Costs and the Rewards will make them look inside to ask Why that Reward is worth fighting for. Later, they'll discover what it is inside them that stands in the way. But for now they have to believe that it's worth the battle.

So how do you do that?

There are a variety of ways to show your character that it's worth the battle:

Give them a hero. Someone who has been the course and fought the good fight, who knows the Reward. Like Obi-Wan Kenobi, who was the Jedi knight and Luke's mentor. Or in *Sleepless in Seattle*, Annie's parents, who had a long-lasting true love.

Give them a glimpse of the darkness. Up the ante by adding into the mix the "what if we do nothing?" question. Give them a glimpse of what could happen if they don't fight the good fight. For example, at the end of *The Fellowship of the Ring*, Frodo and his friends fight Mordor's army. They know the Orcs will overrun the land if they don't stop it. It's sort of a "reverse reward," because we know if they don't succeed, everything will fall apart.

Give them a cause. Kidnap their sidekick, make them fall in love with the princess, save a kingdom—anything to make them realize that if they give up, they'll lose what they love. *Titanic* is a classic example. Falling in love makes Rose realize what she has to live for.

Give them an example. Maybe someone else around them has already achieved the reward. Have the characters look to this person and see that the reward is worth the fight.

Give them a what-if conversation. What if we win the battle and kill all the zombies? We see this a lot, especially in war movies—what if we win? What will we do when we get home? This helps your reader and character visualize the reward and makes the fight worth the cost.

The Reward has to be at least as vivid, as compelling, and as tangible as the Cost, or your hero will put down his sword and go home, back to Act 1.

And that's the wrong direction.

Attempt and Mini-victory

So far we've covered our hero's goal and desire. He's calculated Cost versus Reward, and he's made his attempt to achieve his goal. And he failed. If he is going to go forward, he needs some encouragement. Let's return to our football game we used earlier.

The last time we checked in, the team was huddling up after a disastrous play. However, they risk running the ball because they don't have the blocking they need, not unless the QB blocks. But if he does, their QB might get hurt. Their last four passes were incomplete, so they risk wasting another play. We have here the Risk and Cost of the next play.

What is their Reward? We mentioned they were on the twenty-yard line and six points down, with a minute left on the board, close enough to score. And if they win this game, they'll go to the state playoffs. Maybe there are even banners along the field, fluttering in the wind, reminding them of last year when they won. They have a title to defend.

Now comes what we call the Attempt and Mini-victory. You want to give your character a taste of triumph. Not the entire victory, but enough for him to believe he could achieve it.

In our football scenario, our team runs the sweep, the QB blocks for the tailback, and they achieve the first down. Not a touchdown, but enough to give them a taste of victory looming ten yards away. Maybe the QB gets hurt, but not so much he's taken out of the game, he'll have to dig deep in this next section of the game (and change and grow!) to achieve the win.

This moment gives your character the drive and momentum to dive into Act 2B, the Fight.

However, without this taste of Victory, with the Cost being so high, the rewards fading, your character just might turn around and head for the locker room. Before your character can jump into the fight, he must take a good look at himself. Writing teacher James Scott Bell calls this the *Man in the Mirror Moment*. (His book *Write Your Novel From the Middle* is required reading for all novelists!) I like to add in that glimpse of the hero's Secret Desire—because we're motivated not only by the person we see in the mirror but also the people we want to be.

In his Man in the Mirror Moment, a scene that divides Act 2 in half, a character "sees" himself. Sees his fears, his flaws, and his inadequacies, as well as sees his greatest desires in front of him, and in that moment, he must make his final fight-or-flee decision.

Armed with knowledge of the Cost, the glimpse of the Reward, the taste of Victory, he must look deep inside and ask: *What do I really want? What are my deepest, secret desires?* It's this Secret Desire that propels him forward into the Fight.

Let's take a look at the *The Bourne Identity*. Jason Bourne is on the run, trying to discover who he is. Not only that, he quickly finds out he's being chased. He meets Marie along the way, a girl we don't know much about except that she, too, seems to be alone.

He pays Marie to drive him to France, but once they are there, she's free to go.

Marie's character has a clear taste of desire on their trip, wondering who this man is. He's exciting, as well as uniquely vulnerable. She's intrigued as much as she's afraid. Marie's second attempt to free herself from him is thwarted when Bourne looks at her right before a car chase scene and says, "Are you in or are you out?"

Maria has to decide if the Cost (her life maybe) is worth the Reward (discovering the heart of this man). At this moment, she looks inside herself, asks what she really wants, and reaches for her seatbelt.

She sets aside her caution and fear to stay with him. We witness her character's growth and change.

One of my favorite Man in the Mirror scenes happens in the movie *The Secret Life of Walter Mitty*. Mitty, charged with finding a lost picture, must choose between taking a perilous ride on a helicopter with a drunk pilot or returning to his small, gray life of failure. Danger versus safety. Mitty has lived his life in safety, but deep inside he wants to live a life of adventure, something we've seen in many vignettes up to this point, including a story of how he wanted to backpack across Europe. In a wonderful moment of Character Change, Mitty abandons safety for adventure and embraces the danger of this moment by leaping aboard the chopper as it lifts off the ground.

Now he's ready for the epic fight of his life as he becomes a New Man.

Use the SEQ to plot these key Act 2A elements:

- Attempt/Failure—His attempt at the Noble Quest goal (and Character Change) and Failure.

- Cost—What will the Quest cost him?

- Reward—What will he gain if he succeeds?

- Attempt/Mini-Victory—His second attempt at the Noble Quest goal and a hint of victory.

- Desire/Man in the Mirror—The character must look at himself and recognize not only his Flaws and Fears, but his Greatest/Secret Desire pushing him forward.

Now, girded by the deep motivation, or the Cause embodied in Act 2A, your character is ready to move on to Act 2B, the Fight.

The Fight
Plotting the destruction of your character

The Fight (for Character Change!)

So far we've discussed Acts 1 and 2A, showing your character his need for change, as well as the Cost and Reward of his goal. You've given him a taste of victory and stirred up a desire inside him to keep going despite the sacrifice and challenge ahead.

Now, as you plunge into Act 2B, it's time for your character to Fight. This is the fun part of the book! You, as the author, are going to put your character through a number of skills tests. Interpersonal challenges. Physical foibles. Through these challenges, you'll see him change.

You've Got Mail is a great example of this Fight concept. Remember when Joe Fox is about to meet Kathleen Kelly for the first time in the coffee shop and he realizes that she is his nemesis from The Shop Around the Corner? He then tells Kathleen that he has a project that will need some "tweaking" before they can get together.

The next forty-five minutes or so of the movie are about that tweaking. He proceeds to woo her offline, hoping she'll fall for him in the flesh. But he also woos her online, hoping that when she discovers he is her nemesis, she won't reject him. It's a delicate balance, which makes for fun scenarios, but most of all, both of them realize that they need to change their perspectives if they hope to find true love.

Your character will have some failures during this section. Some slammed doors, maybe some cuts and bruises, but eventually, they will grow stronger, wiser, more heroic. He will fight his fears, be faced with his flaws, be challenged physically and emotionally, and become a stronger person.

Eventually, you're going to give him a string of victories until he feels empowered and powerful. Then, of course, you're going to rip the rug from under him and push him right into his Black Moment.

In my PJ Sugar series, my character, a wannabe PI, struggles with jumping to conclusions that lead her down rabbit trails. But during this Fight phase, I have her get a number of things right and use her sleuthing skills well until she thinks she's practically Sherlock Holmes. Of course, that's when the *real* bad guy shows up . . .

The Fight stage can be plotted by looking first at the external goals and asking: What external obstacles stand in the way? I try to find three obstacles, each one larger with more stakes attached, to challenge the hero.

I sometimes refer to these obstacles as Disappointment, Disaster, and Destruction, just to help me to remember to make each one worse. I reserve Devastation for the Black Moment Event.

Going into each scene during this section ask yourself: What losses can my character(s) have? What victories?

Then ask: What does my hero learn in this scene that makes him a stronger/better person?

The key to this Fight section is to give your hero a taste of victory, enough to keep him from giving up. Ideally, right before the Black Moment Event he'll experience a great triumph. A skirmish won, or perhaps a kiss from the girl. Whatever you can do to make the hero feel that the goal is in his grasp.

And that's when the Black Moment occurs. And Act 3 begins.

The Power of the Black Moment

How then shall I go forward?

A character at the crux of his Black Moment needs to ask "How shall I go forward?" Think back to your SEQ. We talked about a character's Greatest Fear, what caused it, and then used that to create the Black Moment. Every character's Black Moment will be different, uniquely crafted to suit him and bring him to his lowest place.

Why is this Black Moment so important? Because we want him to examine *why* this is his lowest place and to confront the beliefs—especially that spiritual Lie—that has pushed him through life to this dark place.

As he sits in this darkness, he needs to search for truth, the light, so to speak. He'll be looking for an Epiphany, which is the next stage of character growth. The Epiphany should be a Truth, a realization, and something that touches the core of his beliefs.

The key here is to create a Black Moment Event that assaults his values. What does he believe? What drives him?

For example, in my book *Nothing but Trouble*, my character PJ Sugar believes that she is faulty, that she just can't help but get into trouble. This is confirmed in her Black Moment by being accused of a crime she didn't commit (even though all signs point to her guilt). Not only that, but because of her actions, her nephew's life is in danger, and the man she loves believes that she is guilty. She realizes she has to stop believing she is flawed and start living in the truth that God delights in her, despite her cracks. She has an entire paradigm shift, which allows her to see herself and the world differently. And of course, recognize the real culprit.

So make your Black Moment as black as you can by asking: How can I devastate my character? Because on his knees is the perfect place to change his heart and mind. And finally see the light.

The Essential Epiphany

The Epiphany—the grand finale of the inner journey

The Epiphany is the point of your character's journey. Without it, the reader has simply been watching your poor character suffer needlessly.

You must give him a moment of awareness, of change, and of growth, even if it is small.

Why do you need this? Because this is when the Truth will come in and set him free.

How do we deliver that Epiphany? Here are some ideas:

Gradual "light" turning on, naturally, over time. Have your character make a series of small changes that lead to the big change. Then have him stand in a place where his destructive behavior might be repeated and have him see his change—or have someone see the change for him. For example, you could have him "test the truth" a number of times and see gradual changes until he finally gets to a place where he can look back and see the difference of who he was then and who he is now.

The Big "Bang!" Method. Suddenly, your character is at his lowest, and Lie and the Voice of Truth flood back to him and he "gets" it. You've seen this in movies—a montage of pivotal moments that runs through a character's mind. You can do this in books, too—italicized snippets of conversations or a memory of an event seen in a different light. In my book *Nothing but Trouble*, PJ replays her mother's voice in her head—the lies—and I juxtaposed what her mother *really* meant—the Truth.

The Reader *Aha!* **Method.** This is where protagonist doesn't realize his change, but the readers see it. At the end, have him do something he would have never done in the beginning to epitomize the change for the reader. In the thriller *Eagle Eye,* the Epiphany employed this method. The hero never realizes how far he's come—he just jumps right in. But we, as the viewers, understand the change.

The Wakeup Call or "Oh No, Am I Like Him?" I love this method because it is often the one used in our lives. That moment when we look at someone and we realize that we are *them*. The hero sees himself in reality and how much he is like the villain or someone he despises. This jolts him into change. Sometimes this can be separated into two sections: he recognizes the Lie. but then later realizes he needs help to change.

However you choose to deliver the Epiphany, it should be logical and strong enough for your character to realize the Truth and decide to change. Something must "click" for him, and in that moment, he becomes a New Man.

Now that our hero has confronted his Black Moment and seen the light, we've come to the last step of Character Change: the New Man. The changed person he has become, complete with new skills, new beliefs, and new courage.

But it's not enough to want it. Or think it. The reader needs to see it.

The Final Battle

Wrapping up the Inner Journey for Your Hero

Just to reiterate, without the Black Moment there is no point to the journey of your character, no moment of change. It's in the Black Moment that your character discovers why he's gone on this journey. It's also when he learns he must change in order to get what he wants or to accomplish the goal he set out to do at the beginning of the story.

Now that our hero has confronted his Black Moment and seen the light, then we're nearly ready to finish our story. But we have to know that he's changed, that the Black Moment and the Epiphany have worked, and that our character has truly learned his lesson.

How do we show this? There are a number of key elements you'll want to weave into the last section of the book—let's say the last two to three chapters—that will help you prove this.

First, we want to see that your hero is truly a New Man. It's the confirmation and presentation of the changed person he has become, complete with new skills, new beliefs, and new courage.

This New Man moment happens right before the finale of the story. We want to glimpse what our New Man looks like.

A great example is in *Independence Day.* In the Black Moment, our heroes are trapped in the alien ship when they can't disengage and after uploading the virus. They realize that they have to sacrifice their lives, and that it's worth it—something that the scientist, Levinson, wasn't ready to do at the beginning of the movie. Only then are they willing to shoot off the rocket and race for their lives out of the ship against all odds. But first, we see the new men. They sit down in the ship and smoke a cigar together. This is their New Man moment. It's brief, but it shows us who we are rooting for.

Now your character is ready for the finale. The test of the New Man through the Final Battle.

The Final Battle is the section where they test their change. It's the cementing that yes, the Truth is *right,* and with it they can win the day.

The Final Battle, which is not a real battle, but just a metaphor for the concepts, has five parts:

- Storming the Castle
- Lie
- Loss
- Reminder
- Victory

Step One: Storming the Castle

I like to use *The Patriot* here because the finale is an actual battle and fits my metaphor well.

Armed with the Truth, your character will face his last challenge. In that last challenge, he'll come face to face with the Lie, falter, and then forge ahead in Victory. So your character must Storm the Castle. You need to give your hero something he must do. A proactive event that will challenge his Truth. Maybe it's a confrontation, or a declaration, or a surrender, or a challenge . . . whatever it might be, it has to be something that will test his mettle, and that he would not have done at the beginning of his journey.

In *The Patriot*, Benjamin Martin's militia is asked to fight on the line. It's not normally what the militia does—and admittedly, it's a bit crazy. Stand there and let the enemy shoot at you? But this is their task, and Martin convinces them it's worth it.

In my book *Nothing but Trouble*, the first PJ Sugar book, PJ's Black Moment occurs when she is arrested for a crime she didn't commit. She wants to run. But she has learned God made her with a curious mind and all her crazy skills are a good thing. So she returns to pick up her nephew from where he is staying. There she finds the final clue of the mystery, and instead of giving up, she takes a chance, digs deep into her toolkit of skills, and saves the day. It confirms that she's a different person.

I often figure out how characters will Storm the Castle by asking: What can't they do at the beginning of the book that they can at the end? For PJ, it's keeping her commitments. For Benjamin Martin, it's fighting honorably.

Now that we have the Battle overview and the Storm the Castle action, we have to add some conflict. Because only in conflict do we test/reveal the mettle of a man (or woman!).

The next thing we must do to test our character in the Final Battle is to resurrect the Lie.

Step 2: Resurrection of the Lie

Your hero has to believe that he will lose this Final Battle. This is where the Lie raises its almost-dead head. We see it again and we wonder is it going to win or is our man truly a New Man, armed with the Truth, willing to escape and defeat the Lie?

In *The Patriot*, the line falters as the battle ensues, and the militia begins to retreat. Benjamin Martin's Lie is that wars cannot be fought with honor, and clearly, when the militia starts to retreat, this is proven true. The Lie has started to rise again, and it just might be confirmed.

PJ Sugar fails in her attempt to subdue the villain and finds herself in trouble. She's *not* amazing; she's just a mess. That's the Lie. Right on the heels of the resurrection of the Lie is a glimpse of what they might lose.

Step 3: Glimpse of the Loss

With the rising of the Lie there is also the ultimate loss of the goal. The realization that the victory could pass out of your hero's reach.

For example, as the line falters, Benjamin Martin sees Tavington—the man who killed both of his sons. Martin is running forward to kill him when he realizes that his men are fleeing. So he has to make a choice: Does he go after Tavington or help his men stay in the fight?

If he goes after Tavington, the Lie is true—he's only ruthless and thirsty for revenge, and there is no honor in war. If he doesn't, he loses his chance to fight. This is his Loss.

For PJ, if she's killed, the villain will also hurt her nephew, whom she has sworn to protect. She'll have betrayed her sister's love and her mother's confidence. She really will be *Nothing but Trouble*.

Give us a Glimpse of the Loss, and then follow it quickly with a reminder of the Truth.

Step 4: Reminder of the Truth

At the pivotal moment, the hero has to remember the Truth and what he's learned. Just like all of us hear the Voice of Truth that stops us right before we do something we know is wrong, the Truth stops our hero.

In *The Patriot* in a very metaphorical moment, Benjamin Martin sees the flag on the ground. Remember, the flag represents honor, and it was used in the Truth/Epiphany moment earlier. And because of that reminder, our hero chooses Truth, throws down his weapon, and grabs the flag. Then he turns and calls his men back to action, choosing honor over revenge.

Although PJ Sugar has failed at her first attempt, she knows the truth about the mystery and blurts out the plot to the killer. He accuses her of babbling and pounces on her—but this acts as a diversion so the good guys can burst in. She's saved the day with her crazy, everyday skills.

This Reminder of the Truth is the key to cementing that Character Change and leads us to Victory.

Step 5: The Victory!

We must end, of course, with Victory! In *The Patriot,* with the troops rallied, Benjamin Martin is free to fight Tavington, having defeated the Lie and realizing he can choose honor over the bloodthirsty man he's been.

PJ Sugar, having saved the day with her crazy skills, doesn't have to run from her past anymore. She's a heroine in her town.

Do you have a Final Battle? Return to your SEQ and look at what your character wants. Has he achieved this? In the end, Benjamin Martin killed the man who killed his sons—but he did it with honor. Has your character overcome his Flaw? In the end, PJ Sugar refused to give in to her urges to give up and flee, pushing people out of her life.

This is Victory. But we also need a Perfect Ending.

The Happily Ever After Ending

We all love the perfect happy ending, right?

But how do you find that perfect ending? Especially after a journey wrought with trials and loss?

The Happily Ever After (HEA) ending is about giving your character an unexpected joy. Not just a plot victory, which frankly he might not achieve, but a victory that touches the core of who he is and epitomizes his change as a character as well as his accomplishments in the plot. It's about healing the great Wound perpetrated by the Dark Moment so he can finally live Happily Ever After. Think of it this way: the HEA ending is one part Wound Healing, one part Greatest Dream.

Which, of course, you've figured out from your SEQ.

Let's start with the right questions. Remember when we were building characters and we asked our character to tell us his DMS? We pulled out of that the Lie and the Greatest Fear and used those to create the Inner Journey and the Black Moment Event.

We also found the Wound. It could be rejection, or betrayal, or even grief. Often, it has to do with a broken relationship. Our characters carry these wounds around with them, keeping them away from people who might reopen the wound or pour salt in it. This is why our protagonists self-sabotage relationships or veer away from anything substantial—their wounds simply won't allow them to draw close to others for the fear of reopening wounds.

In a romance. this is the key to the romantic journey. The hero and heroine have both been wounded in their past. Sometimes it comes from a previous relationship; maybe it comes from a mistake they've made, or even something that has happened in their family. The key, however, is that this Wound is not only what they will protect but also what they long to heal.

The Wound is where you start to build your HEA ending. You've already done the hard work of finding the DMS. Now go back to the SEQ and ask: What Wound was opened? It can be a derivative of the Lie they believe. Or it might be something different. It could also be that this moment hasn't created a deep enough Wound, and you'll need to create another one. You can do this, but you'll have to apply the same principles—writing it out, telling another character about it in your story. It can get complicated to have more than one DMS, so that's why I suggest focusing on one DMS. However if you are writing a romance, having a separate Romantic DMS can often work well.

What do Romantic Wounds look like? Maybe our hero had a girl-friend in college who betrayed him with his roommate. The Fear of betrayal, then, keeps him from love, and the Lie he believes, to keep this simple, is that he is unlovable. Obviously, you want to dig deeper than this to get at the real heart of the Lie, but this works for now. The Wound, of course, is that moment when he realizes his girlfriend chose someone else. This sense of rejection is what will be healed in the story.

As we apply this to our HEA ending, we need to start by asking: What is your deep Wound? Why do you hurt? Answering these questions helps you as the author know what you need to heal.

For example, if we were to use another one of my favorite movies, *Return to Me*, the hero states his Wound right out: He will always miss his wife, but he aches for Grace. He aches for that person who fills up his life, completes him. We see this Wound appearing in his DMS, when he arrives home after his first wife's death, takes the dog in his arms, and says, "She's not coming back. She gone." The Wound is visibly played out in subsequent scenes when we see that her absence has played destruction on his personal life, turning his apartment to shambles. He is lost without his wife—until he finds Gracie. And when she leaves him, reopening the Wound, he voices it.

Healing the Wound is only one component of the HEA ending. Now you need to give us that sigh of contentment at the end of the story, that moment of delight not just for the character, but for the reader. You do this by utilizing your character's Greatest Dream.

The Greatest Dream isn't just about healing the Wound or winning the day or conquering his Fear. It's something deeper, sometimes something your character won't even know or understand.

Let's go back to *Return to Me* as an example.

The hero's Happiest Moment is on the dance floor in the scene right before his wife is killed. It epitomizes how they belong together. The Greatest Dream for the hero, of course, is to have his wife back. But we know he'll never have that. The author, however, can delight him and the reader by giving him a piece of his Greatest Dream with a woman who has the heart of his wife, both literally and figuratively.

Let's look at the heroine, Gracie. Her Happiest Moment is getting her donor heart, but she also realizes that it cost someone dearly. Her Greatest Dream is to thank the person who gave her the heart and to live a good life, worthy of such a gift. The author delights her and us by allowing her to "give" the hero a little something of his wife and to know that he feels she is worthy of this gift.

The HEA ending is a combination of Healing the Wound (for Gracie, being accepted despite the Cost, and for the hero, allowing himself to love again) and the Greatest Dream.

How do you find the Greatest Dream?

Start by asking: What is your character's Happiest Moment in his past?

We want to dig around in his past to find that one moment when everything worked, everything was right. And we want to extrapolate from that some element that we can then use in the ending.

Just like when you interviewed your character to discover his DMS, don't let him give a simple answer like "When I graduated from college" or "When I got married." Make him retell a specific story. You want to pinpoint an exact event with details. An exact event allows you to take a good look at it, and, if you want, recreate it. Most of all, it allows you to find the minute nuances that pull out exactly why this was the Happiest Moment.

Maybe it is when, standing in the rain with her father at the carnival, the heroine's hopes for a sunny, bright day are ruined until he takes her hand. It's that warmth, holding her steady, that she loves. Her Happiest Moment is knowing she's not alone in the storms of life.

Now, if your character just can't come up with a happy moment, then try asking: What do you want more than anything and why? Often the *Why* will lead to the moment you are looking for. (This is the Secret Desire, something you discovered when you drew your SEQ.)

Here's the important part: Make your character write it down in detail. I prefer to write it in first person because then it feels like a conversation. I can ask questions, and I can hear the inflection and emotion in his voice. It feels more real in first person and brings it onto the page. You'll also use this passage in a number of ways in the story.

How to use this Greatest Dream for the most impact

First, you want to pull from this story the nuances or pieces of the story that you might be able to give your character. For example, in one of my early books, *Happily Ever After*, my character Joe's Happiest Moment was fishing with his father. Unfortunately, his father walked out on his family, but Joe still remembers the companionship, the shared joy of netting a fish with someone he loves. So I sent Joe fishing with his brother and gave him that same sense of companionship. It's enough of a taste of happiness that it gives Joe the courage to find his father, forgive him, and restore their broken relationship.

Pull one element of the Happiest Moment out and see if you can recreate it or give him that Greatest Dream in some way.

Second, you want to make sure the reader knows what the Greatest Dream is, or at least what the Happiest Moment is. Why? Because when we know each other's greatest dreams, we want to make them come true. We also bond with the hero in the retelling of the story. (Much like how we use the DMS.)

During Act 2, the retelling of the Happiest Moment is a powerful tool to bond your reader with your characters. You don't always have to use it to bond the hero and heroine. If you are not writing a romance, it might be between two male friends, or a woman and her daughter, or it could even be with a stranger. The key is to tell the story in dialogue, not narrative, to make it powerful.

Finally, be creative. This is where you can make sure your ending is not predictable. What surprise ending can you give the hero from your analysis of the Happiest Moment? Not just the appearance of someone influential in his life, but what about a unique job opportunity, or a discovery of some unique talent, or perhaps a secret that allows him to live a better life? In *The Patriot,* the HEA ending includes Benjamin Martin's compatriots surprising him by rebuilding his burnt down house. What he wants in the movie is redemption. What he receives is not just redemption but respect.

Creating the Happily Ever After thread

How do you weave in the HEA thread without making it obvious and yet making sure it is believable? Here are a few techniques:

First: Give us a Glimpse! Remember in Act 1 when we gave our hero a glimpse of his Greatest Dream? He probably didn't even realize it (nor did the reader, until now). Nevertheless, it sits in the back of his brain and he recognizes it as he digs deep in the Desire moment of Act 2 and realizes this is the reason to continue his journey.

This also means that you must hint at the possibility of the hero achieving his Greatest Dream early in Act 2 as a way to motivate him on his journey. Give him another glimpse of it, or have someone tell him that it is possible. (Ah, the Reward!)

You want to hint just enough to alert him to the fact that yes, he can have it all if he just keeps going.

I hope you're not tired of my examples from *The Patriot* yet, because I have one more. There are so many layers in this movie, but one of the happiest moments for Benjamin Martin is his family and the wife he loved. He gets a glimpse that happy endings are possible when he sees Gabriel falling in love with Anne in the moment where they share the inky tea smiles.

It's important now to keep both the reader and the character guessing so you can surprise them with the HEA ending. You do this by killing the dream, or the hope of it, during the Black Moment. It might be a literal death, like Anne's and Gabriel's deaths, or it might be figurative, something that the hero will lose, like the woman he loves walking away, or the death of a job, or failure in battle. Something that makes him believe that all of his dreaming is for naught.

Of course then you'll surprise him by giving him some powerful element of the Greatest Dream at the end.

So, let's sum up. To find the HEA ending, you must discover the two elements that will knit it together: the healing of the Wound and the delivery of the Greatest Dream.

You find this Happily Ever After ending by doing two things:

Determine the Wound. What would heal this?

Determine the Greatest Dream. What part of this can you, as the author, give him?

A great book leaves the character and the reader both healed and delighted. Give them an ending they can't forget.

And one that makes them pass the book along.

Section Five
You Can Write a Brilliant Story!

From SEQ to Plot: How to Create Your Own SEQ

So there you are, staring at the blank page and wondering how to start your story. You have a story idea, and the hope that you'll be able to bring all your ideas to fruition, Or maybe you don't have a plethora of ideas . . . just a wild hope and a blank page.

You can do this. Remember, the SEQ starts with one simple question: *Who are you?*

Start with an adjective and a noun. From there, drill down, asking, "*Why?*" until you come to a powerful, relatable, poignant Dark Moment Story (DMS).

Have your character tell you this story in detail in first person. Write it down. You'll use it to create the character, the rough plot, and as a bonding device when it is told in dialogue between characters in the story.

Once you have the DMS, pull out all the SEQ ingredients:

The Greatest Fear—which you'll use to build the *Black Moment Event* in Act 3. You'll also use it to build your character *Flaw*. This will help you figure out his behavior at the beginning and his *New Man* change at the end, culminating in that thing he can do at the end that he can't at the beginning, usually a *Sacrifice* or *Grand Gesture*, and often shown during the *Final Battle*.

The Lie your character believes—this sets up his inner journey. You'll use the Lie to form the final *Epiphany* (Truth) as well as truthlets dropped by secondary characters or derived from action in the story. The Lie also molds his motivations and choices from the onset of the story. The power of the Lie is realized during the *Black Moment Effect* to set up the *Epiphany* and cause inner Character Change.

The Wound—the emotional repercussion of the DMS. This Wound is used in the formation of the Happily Ever After (HEA) ending, as well as used in a romance to create the Breakup. The Wound also causes healing between characters.

The Secret Desire—used to create the inner motivation for the Noble Quest. Awakened by the Inciting Incident, the Secret Desire is something birthed after the DMS and nested deep inside the hero. It is the primary motivation behind his Noble Quest.

Add to these primary elements:

Competing Values—two powerful values, birthed from his DMS, which compete to push the character forward, especially during the Great Debate. In Act 2, these values will propel him forward in turns until the Black Moment Event when he usually must choose between one or the other to complete the story (and thus contribute to the Black Moment Effect).

Want—the motivation behind the external goal, a clearer, articulated driving force that propels the character forward from the first scene. The Want is transformed by the Inciting Incident and the

Invitation to the Noble Quest into an external, Specific, Measurable, Attainable, Realistic and Timely (SMART) goal.

Once external goals are established, obstacles can be brainstormed to discover the external conflict.

Why—the simple motivation behind his actions, the culmination of the DMS in an easy explanation. This motivation keeps you, as the author, centered on why he's taking this journey.

Happiest Moment—although this is not part of the DMS, this helps build the Greatest Dream and sets up the perfect HEA ending. Similar to the DMS, it should be relatable, specific, poignant, and used in the story to bond the characters together in the retelling.

Once you've put together your SEQ with all the elements, create a rough LINDY HOP and plug in the "bookends" of your story—the Act 1 elements (Life, Inciting Incident, Noble Quest) and Act 3 elements (Help—Black Moment Event/Effect, Overhaul—Epiphany/New Man, Perfect Ending—Wound Healing/Greatest Dream).

Then it's time to work on Act 2A, adding in the Attempt/Failure, Cost-Reward, Attempt/Mini-victory, Desire/Man in the Mirror to build the Cause. Then in Act 2B, your character will Fight for his Cause, and you'll craft three to four big plot obstacles (Disappointment, Disaster, Destruction) leading up to the high moment right before the Devastation (Black Moment Event).

You'll layer in the Fear, Lie, and Flaw in Act 1, the truthlets, Competing Values (and more flaws, fears, and lies), as well as the DMS and Happiest Moment story in Act 2, and create the Final Battle for Act 3, the climax of the story, including a Grand Gesture or Sacrifice, that thing he can do at the end that he can't at the beginning.

The story will end with the perfect HEA ending that heals Wound and gives your hero something of his Greatest Dream.

And then, you'll do it all over again for your heroine or any other protagonists in your story, merging their stories. Often I think it helps to create the SEQs for all my POV characters and then build the plot once I can see each character's story.

If that sounds overwhelming, I have a one-hour webinar that explains this process and breaks it down step-by-step. And it's free in my *Introduction to the SEQ* course.

Now you have the ingredients to begin to build your plot from the inside out. And it all adds up to a brilliant novel.

Your brilliant novel. Because your story matters.

Now go, **Write Something Brilliant!**

Thank you for reading The Story Equation!

I hope this has been helpful for you! We at My Book Therapy believe your story matters, and we're privileged to help you on your writing journey.

If you'd like to learn more about how to build a powerful novel using The Story Equation, including how to create a Character Change Journey and the secrets to building Scene Tension, visit www.learnhowtowriteanovel.com. And for classes on how to get published and stay published, visit www.novel.academy.

Would you like a free infographic and 1-hour lesson on how to build a powerful character?

Check out our Story Equation Mini-Course!
(http://novel.academy/courses/TheSEQ/)

About the Author

Susan May Warren

is the RITA award-winning, best-selling author of over fifty novels. With over a million books sold, Susan has won the Christy award twice, and been a finalist eight times. She is also a multi-time winner of the Inspirational Reader's Choice contest and the ACFW Carol Award. She specializes in characterization and has won acclaim for her gripping stories and suspenseful plots. Susan teaches on writing at conferences around the nation and is the founder of www.MyBookTherapy.com, www.LearnHowToWriteANovel.com, and Novel.Academy, all resources for helping aspiring writers.

More writing resources by Susan May Warren

How to Write a Brilliant Novel

Have you always wanted to write a novel but didn't know where to start? This book is for you. With proven techniques, easy to understand explanations, and practical steps, from the Inside . . . Out will teach you how a story is structured and then take you through the process of creating and marketing your novel.

Topics include:

- Character-driven plotting,
- How to HOOK your reader,
- Elements and flow of scenes,
- How to build storyworld,
- Secrets to sizzling dialogue,
- Proven self-editing techniques,
- Synopsis and query letter writing,
- How to manage your writing career—and everything in between!

Conversations with a Writing Coach

Empowering. Essential. Fun. You made the dream real.

These are words used to describe the conversations Susan May Warren had with students over the decade. Writing books are helpful, but they can be overwhelming and challenging to understand. Sometimes all writers need is someone to sit down beside them, believe in them, and patiently walk through the novel creation process, step-by-step. Now you can join the conversation as Susie discusses high-level story pitches, how to decide what story to write, character creation and story structure, and an easy method to creating a story summary. She covers scene building and how to create tension, then goes deeper with emotional layering, storyworld, and dialogue. Most of all, each conversation is delivered as if the student is sharing a cup of coffee, the language and explanations accessible. Writers will sit down with an idea . . . and leave with a novel.

Excerpt from Conversations:

Conversation #1: So you want to be a writer.

I agreed to meet Sally at the local coffee shop on a Monday morning, and I told her to bring a notebook. I'd seen her at church a few times with her four children hanging on her like she might be monkey bars. She ran the children's program and had even pulled off the church Christmas musical with twenty haloed children in under a month, so I knew she had the energy as well as the chops to make it happen if she wanted it.

She wanted to write a novel.

I told her that over the next year, I would be glad to help get all the way to a finished manuscript. She simply needed to be willing to hear the truth and dare to take my advice.

I sat there nursing my extra-tall latté, watching the snow peel from the sky, the drifts lining the rocky shoreline outside the window, and remembering my own journey, started in Siberia, Russia. Armed with just a desire to write a novel, I began to pull books off my shelves and study the masters.

Forty-five novels, later, I am still amazed at the journey. I've learned a few things, made a number of mistakes, and taken a few courageous steps. And here I was, looking forward to helping Sally Anderson begin her own journey to become a published author.

She came in five minutes late, wearing a parka, a skier's hat, and carrying a messenger bag, her eyes bright, if not a little nervous. She dumped her bag on the chair and tugged out a three-ring binder. "I brought a sample of my writing," she said, and handed it to me as she went to order her coffee.

I skimmed through her work while I waited. A few newsletters, short stories, a children's play, a number of devotionals. All interesting, if not just a little predictable, the writing solid, even if not engaging. I clearly recognized enough of a voice that, with the right encouragement, might sing.

She had potential. And when she sat down with her moose mocha, enthusiasm. "Thank you for meeting with me! I just love your books. I want to write like you someday."

I handed back her notebook. "I want you to write like you someday," I said with a smile. "Tell me why you want to be a writer."

I wasn't just being polite. I have found as I've taught writing across the world that there are different types of novelists. There are those who have a message and want to change the world by communicating it through a novel. These folks are zealous, but they aren't always writers – sometimes they are simply evangelists, and writing a book seems the easiest way to get their message out. I fear for them, because they can become easily discouraged when they see other books written on their topic. Or, if their book, which they've worked so hard on, (and which has such a great message) is turned down by an agent.

Then there are those who have endured incredible suffering or struggles and are seeking to make sense of it through a gripping novel. Maybe, if they write a best-seller, their suffering will serve a purpose. I try to help them see the other side—the part where people might not appreciate their suffering, and in fact, the Amazon reviews might only cause more struggle (because even if there are thousands of great reviews, the few negative ones will eat away at their peace of mind). To these folks I say, "You didn't suffer so you could write a book. And your novel won't suddenly justify your struggles. You have to find that answer, that peace somewhere else." Here's some truth: If you aren't happy with who you are before you're published, you won't suddenly find inner peace after you're published. Sometimes being published can actually make that peace even a little more elusive.

So, I asked the question with a little intake of my breath, hoping
. . .

"I think story has the power to change lives . . ."

Uh oh.

"I have a number of life experiences that I think would be interesting in a novel, and I think I'm supposed to share them . . ."

I tried not to wince.

"But really, I just can't help but write. I love words and how they
flow together, and I love stories, and spend way too much time
dreaming up plots. I know my kids are little, but I just can't escape
this urge to write. I would do it even if I never got published."

I wanted to give her a little hug, but I didn't want to scare her off.
"Yes. Isaac Asimov said, 'I'd rather write than breathe.' This is the
mark of a true novelist—that idea that you can't turn off the stories,
or the words. You must have this kind of passion to stay the course
of writing a novel, because I promise, there will come a day when
you want to put the pen down and walk away."

She looked dubious.

"Your passion, however, won't let you."

She nodded.

Sally, I could work with. "Do you have a story idea?" I asked, need-
ing a warm-up on my latte.

"Not yet. Can you help me?"

"I can't help you find a story, but I can point you where to look.
Every story starts with a story spark—a great idea generated by
something you see or hear and nurtured by something you care
about. My book, The Shadow of your Smile, was sparked by the
thought of my daughter leaving for college, and what I would do if
something ever happened to her. The story spark acts as your vision

for your novel and generates the Story Question that will drive your reader through your story."

"A story question?"

"We'll get to that. But here's your assignment, if you dare: Write a list of five things you are passionate about. Five things you fear the most. Five things you've always wanted to do, and five interesting things that have made you stop and think in the past couple of weeks. Then apply a 'what if' question to each of those five things."

"I lost my son in the mall for twenty minutes during Christmas."

"Exactly that. What if you hadn't found him? What if someone took him? What if . . . I dunno . . . Santa took him?"

She shuddered.

"But seriously, it's those sorts of situations and questions that can lead to a novel spark. Now that you have the truth about what it takes to write a book--do you have the courage to take the dare?"

She finished her coffee and gathered her notebook. "I'm a mom. What do you think?"

Yes, I liked Sally a lot. I couldn't wait see what she'd come up with.

Truth: Novelists must have a passion for writing and storytelling.

Dare: Write your own lists of five. What Story Spark can you find?

Get Conversations with a Writing Coach!